NO LONGER MERE
MORTALS

NO LONGER MERE
MORTALS

SEVEN SECRETS TO LIVING
THE SUPERNATURAL LIFE

KERRICK BUTLER

Published by Harrison House Publishers

Shippensburg, PA 17257

ISBN 13 TP: 978-1-6803-1847-0

ISBN 13 eBook: 978-1-6803-1848-7

ISBN 13 HC: 978-1-6803-1850-0

ISBN 13 LP: 978-1-6803-1849-4

For Worldwide Distribution, Printed in the U.S.A.

1 2 3 4 5 6 7 8 / 26 25 24 23 22

To my wonderful wife and my amazing children—thank you for your loving support and allowing me the time to pen the message of this book—a message that has been ringing through my soul for decades.

To my Faith family—Faith Christian Center—thank you for your prayerful support. It is an honor and a great joy to serve as your pastor.

To all those who dream that there is more to this life—this book is for you. There is so much more to this life, and I pray that this book helps you to launch out into the journey of the superhuman life.

CONTENTS

INTRODUCTION

It was a warm Sunday evening in Georgia, and I was attending the Sunday night service of the church I would one day pastor. On this day, I did not know that I would one day pastor the church; I was only seven years old. Our pastor was not speaking; instead, our outreach minister was sharing the message on his heart. Over the years, I would know him as a kind man who consistently flowed with the Spirit and operated in the gifts of the Spirit with power. He finished preaching and began to walk the aisles accompanied by his wife and a few others. As he walked the aisles, he prayed for different individuals and flowed in the Spirit with power. As long as I can remember, I was drawn to and amazed by the moving and flowing of God's Spirit. The outreach minister approached the place where I was sitting and asked me to stand up. As I did, he prayed for me, and I sensed the presence of God. As he finished praying, I sat back quickly, knowing I had encountered the presence of God, but feeling unsure how to best explain it.

The next night, my family and I were gathered around the table for dinner. As we were eating, my parents asked me about my experience on Sunday night. As I picked through my food, I did my best to explain that I had sensed the presence of God and sat backwards, but not necessarily fell backwards. From my attempt to explain, my parents probably realized I did not know how to explain the previous night's experience. For the rest of dinner, my parents explained to me the importance of reverencing the move of the Spirit of God.

As I look over my life's journey so far, the lessons I received from my elders, and my own adventures with God, two hallmarks that stand out to me concerning flowing with the Spirit of God are *hunger* and *reverence*. The Spirit of God wants every single believer to flow with Him and operate in His power. As I will share later in this book, one of the ways God's Spirit is described in the Scriptures is as a river. In any stream or river, you can fight against the water, or you can go along with the flow. It is similar when it comes to flowing with the Spirit of God. To flow with God's Spirit is to cooperate with Him, to partner with Him, to fellowship with Him, and to allow Him to operate through you. When we observe the terrain of life, we should see the opportunity to flow with the Holy Spirit as an adventure that we have the privilege to undertake. Every adventure has a beginning. The adventure of flowing in the Spirit begins at the crossroads of hunger and reverence.

Adventures are often known for their heroes; when I was growing up, my house was filled with the heroic exploits of superheroes. My brothers and I collected thousands of comics and hundreds of action figures. Every Saturday morning, my parents would join us as we watched cartoons of our favorite superhero team. We had costumes and video games that allowed us to imagine being our favorite superhero on an adventure to make a difference in their imaginary world.

> The Spirit of God wants every single believer to flow with Him and operate in His power.

Some of our favorite superheroes have become Hollywood legends with billion-dollar box office successes; it seems we are a generation of people who are enthralled by the superhuman actions of these heroes. I wonder whether others have also imagined themselves as superheroes. More than likely, they did.

The human soul longs to reach beyond human limitations and experience a superhuman life. *Superhuman* is an adjective that is defined as "having or showing exceptional ability or powers." What may come as a shock to many people, including Christians, is that God wants us to live a superhuman life. The problems of our day have to be addressed in a superhuman way.

When you made Jesus the Lord of your life, you ceased being a mere mortal. Flowing in the Spirit is an adventurous journey in which you can experience the superhuman life. If you are a Christian, you are no longer a mere mortal; it is time to stop behaving as one. The Spirit of God has so much more for you to experience and accomplish. To experience and accomplish what He has for you, you must begin the adventure.

In this book, I will share seven secrets, or principles, that will help you on this adventurous journey. As you embark on this journey, you will discover that these secrets are not hidden from you, but hidden *for you*. As you walk out this journey, these principles will transform from secrets to revealed truth that you can apply in your everyday life. Let's begin the journey! The adventure of flowing in the Spirit begins at the crossroads of hunger and reverence.

The adventure of flowing in the Spirit begins at the crossroads of hunger and reverence.

SECRET 1

HUNGER

*Blessed are those who hunger
and thirst for righteousness, for
they shall be filled* (MATTHEW 5:6).

"M as! Mas!" the pastor cried out in Spanish.

The congregation joined in the cries, "Mas! Mas!"

I was twenty years old and attending a service at Rey de Reyes, pastored by Claudio Freidzon in Buenos Aires, Argentina. The cries of "Mas!" are translated in English as "More!" They were simply crying out to God, asking Him to pour out more of His power during their time together.

The cries for "Mas!" marked me in a special way, partly because of how much of God's power I had experienced since being with my brothers and sisters in Argentina. The atmosphere of the church was so electrified by the presence of God that you could sense the difference as you walked into the building. During the time I had the privilege of being there, I had watched as the power of God ministered to people, bringing healing, joy, and deliverance.

I was a sophomore at Oral Roberts University and part of the Business Missions Team holding a business seminar at Rey de Reyes. Our team taught business principles, and the presence of God flooded the room. We had thousands of testimonies of people healed by the power of God, people receiving wisdom and God ideas, and people experiencing financial and business increase.

The cries for "Mas!" marked me because I was experiencing one of the greatest displays of the power of God in my life, and the people of God were still asking for more. They were hungry for more of God's presence. Hunger is an important quality when it comes to flowing with God's Spirit, being selected by Him, and being prepared by Him.

In Matthew 5:6, Jesus declared, "Blessed are those who hunger and thirst for righteousness, for they shall be filled." The word for *hunger* metaphorically represents "an intense craving and a passionate, fierce desire." In the same way, *thirst* metaphorically paints the pictures of an individual who is eagerly longing for something. In this Scripture, *righteousness* is defined as "whatever is right, just, and conforms to the revealed will of God."

Flowing with the Spirit of God, partnering with Him, and operating in His power is right and just, and it is the will of God for every single believer. Knowing that this is the will of God, we can boldly assert that if we hunger and thirst to flow with the Spirit, we will be filled. The word for *filled* in this Scripture means "fed and satisfied." You will be satisfied to the degree of your hunger and thirst.

If you have a small desire to flow with God's Spirit, then you will flow with the Spirit of God in a smaller or more limited capacity. If you have a greater hunger and thirst for flowing with the Spirit of God, you will be satisfied and fulfilled with greater opportunities to partner and cooperate with the Holy Spirit. God honors righteous desires and takes great delight in satisfying those who hunger and thirst for what is right.

In John 7:37–38, we find this promise from Jesus:

> *On the last day, that great day of the feast, Jesus stood and cried out, saying, "If anyone thirsts, let him come to Me and drink. He who believes in Me, as the Scripture has said, out of his heart will flow rivers of living water."*

In verse 39, John added an explanation, saying, "But this He spoke concerning the Spirit, whom those believing in Him would receive; for the Holy Spirit was not yet given, because Jesus was not yet glorified" (John 7:39). God had prophesied this event through the prophet Isaiah, saying, "For I will pour water on him who is thirsty, and floods on the dry ground; I will pour My Spirit on your descendants, and My blessing on your offspring" (Isaiah 44:3).

Similarly, in Psalm 107:8–9, the psalmist proclaimed, "Oh, that men would give thanks to the Lord for His goodness, and for His wonderful works to the children of men! For He satisfies the longing soul, and fills the hungry soul with goodness."

Both of these passages show us that the level of your hunger and thirst determines your motivation and your priorities. In the natural, if you are hungry enough, you will stop what you are doing to eat. If you are thirsty enough, you will put this book down and drink a beverage. Hunger and thirst are key factors in our daily decision-making process. As we plan our days, we make time for meals and snacks throughout the day. If we are going on a trip, we bring along what we think will satisfy our hunger and thirst on our journey.

> The level of your hunger and thirst determines your motivation and your priorities.

In the same way, our hunger and thirst for the things of God affects our schedule and priorities. To the degree that you hunger and thirst to flow with the Spirit of God, you will organize your schedule and life around doing what is necessary to partner and cooperate with God in a greater way. Many people do not hunger for more of God, because they do not know there is more for them to experience of Him in this life. Because of this lack of hunger and limited knowledge, they live their Christian lives with little to no power.

It reminds me of one of my favorite TV shows in high school, *Smallville*, which is a coming-of-age story about a teenage Clark Kent growing in his powers and beginning to understand his destiny as Superman. At the beginning of the series, Clark is already stronger and faster than everyone around him; as he matures, he grows even stronger and faster. Yet, this is not the only increase he experiences; he also develops supersonic hearing, heat vision, super breath, x-ray vision, and the ability to fly. What if Clark Kent had stopped growing and contented himself with strength and speed? I'm sure he could have accomplished a lot, but he wouldn't be the iconic Superman that has filled countless books, comics, movies, shows, and stories.

In the same way, many Christians live below their privilege and power because they have not realized what is available to them. What you have experienced thus far is not all that is available; God has more for those who dare to hunger after Him. God honors those who desire what is right and long to flow with His Spirit. I know you have the desire to flow with the Spirit of God simply because you are reading this book. God will honor your desire and satisfy your hunger and thirst for Him.

The Scripture tells us about various people who were hungry and thirsty for God and His ways, people who longed to flow with Him and, as a result, lived a superhuman life. Moses and his successor, Joshua, are two of those people. Moses' hunger for more of God is evident in his famous encounter with God in Exodus 33:13–23:

"Now therefore, I pray, if I have found grace in Your sight, show me now Your way, that I may know You and that I may find grace in Your sight. And consider that this nation is Your people."

And He said, "My Presence will go with you, and I will give you rest."

Then he said to Him, "If Your Presence does not go with us, do not bring us up from here. For how then will it be known that Your people and I have found grace in Your sight, except You go with us? So we shall be separate, Your people and I, from all the people who are upon the face of the earth."

So the Lord said to Moses, "I will also do this thing that you have spoken; for you have found grace in My sight, and I know you by name."

And he said, "Please, show me Your glory."

Then He said, "I will make all My goodness pass before you, and I will proclaim the name of the Lord before you. I will be gracious to whom I will be gracious, and I will have compassion on whom I will have compassion."

But He said, "You cannot see My face; for no man shall see Me, and live." And the Lord said, "Here is a place by Me, and you shall stand on the rock. So it shall be, while My glory passes by, that I will put you in the cleft of the rock, and will cover you with My hand while I pass by. Then I will take away My hand, and you shall see My back; but My face shall not be seen."

The glory of God, His manifested and visible presence, is seen and described in many different ways throughout the Bible. Sometimes the glory is described as brilliant light or a devouring fire. At other times, the glory of God is described as wind, rain, or a bright cloud. The glory of God is synonymous with the Spirit of God and how He manifests His goodness and power.

In this passage, Moses had been continually experiencing a powerful and visible display of the glory of God. The pillar of cloud of the glory descended and stood at the door of the tabernacle. Although this was a wonderful manifestation of God's glory, Moses was hungry for more of God. While encountering the cloud and conversing with God about His presence, Moses asked for more when he said, "Please show me Your glory."

I want you to notice something: God was not angry at Moses' request. He did not reply, "You should be happy with you have. How dare you ask me for more!" God replied, "I will make all My goodness pass before you." The word for *glory* denotes "a heaviness associated with good things, honor, splendor, abundance, and wealth." God's glory is heavy with everything good, which is why God said He would make His goodness pass by Moses.

In Exodus 34, Moses' request was granted. He saw God's hand, His back, and His similitude. This encounter changed Moses; it even affected Him physically. When Moses left the mountain, His face radiated and shone with the glory of God. Moses also had a greater understanding and revelation of God than the rest of Israel.

Psalm 103:7 says that God made known His ways to Moses and His acts to the children of Israel. God's acts were clearly seen, but most of Israel did not understand the ways of God. Moses did. Moses got to understand God's ways and have a marvelous encounter with Him because he was hungry for more of God than he had experienced. His hunger for God opened the door for Him to experience more of God and to be satisfied with God's presence, power, and goodness.

Joshua, Moses' successor, was also hungry for the glory of God. We see that in Exodus 33:

> *And it came to pass, when Moses entered the tabernacle, that the pillar of cloud descended and stood at the door of the tabernacle, and the Lord talked with Moses. All the people saw the pillar of cloud standing at the tabernacle door, and all the people rose and worshiped, each man in his tent door. So the Lord spoke to Moses face to face, as a man speaks to his friend. And he would return to the camp, but his servant Joshua the son of Nun, a young man, did not depart from the tabernacle* (Exodus 33:9–11).

This passage does not portray a one-time event. It happened on a regular basis; as often as Moses came to meet with God, the cloud would descend. As often as the cloud descended, Joshua would stay for an extended period of time in the presence of the Lord. Joshua's willingness to wait in the presence of God for an extended period of time shows his hunger for God, His glory, and His ways. At this point, Joshua's assignment was to assist Moses. When Moses finished meeting with God, Joshua's assignment in the tabernacle had concluded. Joshua's desire for more of God caused him to press past what was required for his assignment. Joshua's hunger displays the beautiful connection between hunger and waiting on the Lord.

> Joshua's desire for more of God caused him to press past what was required for his assignment.

Lamentations 3:25 tells us, "The Lord is good to those who wait for Him, to the soul who seeks Him." To wait on the Lord is to eagerly expect and look for Him. Years ago, I was at a convention with the Reverend Tim Storey, a man God used to help me learn to flow with Him in a greater way. At this convention, Rev. Storey shared important truths about living a miraculous life. In part of his message, he shared about the power of expectation. He recounted a time when he was walking through a neighborhood that, in his own words, "people wanted to get out of before a certain time." He approached a bus stop where people were in great expectation of the bus. The potential passengers were even leaning toward the direction the bus would come from. Rev. Storey asked one of the passengers if he was waiting for the bus. The passenger replied emphatically that he was waiting for the bus, shared the bus' number, and added that it was the last bus for the day. Rev. Storey concluded that we should lean into and expect the miraculous from God just like the people were expecting the bus to come at a certain time.

The waiting side of hunger is not a passive passage of time. The waiting side of hunger is an approach where you earnestly expect God to satisfy your passionate desire for Him whenever and wherever you go. This is the approach you take in your personal prayer time, when reading God's Word, when going to church, when watching church online, or anytime throughout your everyday life. This approach is equivalent to the seeking after the Lord that we see in Lamentations 3:25. When you are hungry for God, you do not mind spending more time waiting on Him; you are not consistently rushing through your time with Him, because you fully believe that what He will satisfy you with is greater than anything else.

King David, in the Bible, knew the power of hunger and waiting upon the Lord. David, as we learn from studying his life, accomplished many superhuman feats. Throughout his psalms, David referenced his passionate, fierce desire for God, His presence, and His glory. In Psalm 63:1–2, David declared:

> *O God, You are my God; early will I seek You; my soul thirsts for You; my flesh longs for You in a dry and thirsty land where there is no water. So I have looked for You in the sanctuary, to see Your power and Your glory.*

To seek God is to long after Him and to turn yourself to Him. *Seek* indicates David's desire and hunger for God. David wrote Psalm 63 when he was in the wilderness of Judah; although he was in the wilderness, he had the glory of God on his mind as he declared that he wanted to see God's power and glory as he had in God's sanctuary. A hunger for God will cause you to want to see God's glory and power displayed no matter where you are.

Similarly, in Psalm 84:2, David wrote, "My soul longs, yes, even faints for the courts of the Lord; my heart and my flesh cry out for the living God." David desired to be in God's presence to such an extent that he described his soul as fainting with desire and longing.

In the famously quoted Psalm 42:1–2, David wrote,

> *As the deer pants for the water brooks, so pants my soul for You, O God. My soul thirsts for God, for the living God. When shall I come and appear before God?*

Let the vivid imagery David poetically shared fill your soul. In the same way a deer needs and pursues water from a brook, David chased after God.

Likewise, in Psalm 143:6, David said, "I spread out my hands to You; my soul longs for You like a thirsty land." Imagine a land that has be without rain for a significant period of time and is stricken with drought. How much would the people, the animals, and the land itself need rain? In the same way, David described his need for God.

Even further, in Psalm 27:13–14, he proclaimed:

I would have lost heart, unless I had believed that I would see the goodness of the Lord in the land of the living. Wait on the Lord; be of good courage, and He shall strengthen your heart; wait, I say, on the Lord!

As I shared before, waiting on God is a lifestyle in which you earnestly expect God to satisfy your passionate desire for Him whenever and wherever you go. David waited on God from a place of great desire for Him and fully expected to see God display His goodness in His life. This expectation caused David to continue to move forward in life and not faint and quit. David's example encourages us that waiting upon the Lord is a key to being strengthened. Waiting on the Lord was a powerful force for good in the life of King David. As he shared in Psalm 130:5, "I wait for the Lord, my soul waits, and in His word I do hope."

> Praising and worshipping God is a way to keep our minds focused on Him and keep our expectation in God.

As we conclude our look at David, it's good to remember that all of these verses about hunger and waiting on the Lord were written to music. This reveals another key to waiting on God—praise and worship. Praising and worshipping God is a way to keep our minds focused on Him and keep our expectation in God. Leaders in the early church knew this to be true as well. Acts 13 tells about a time when a group of ministers gathered together to wait on God and hear from Him:

> *As they ministered to the Lord and fasted, the Holy Spirit said, "Now separate to Me Barnabas and Saul for the work to which I have called them." Then, having fasted and prayed, and laid hands on them, they sent them away* (Acts 13:2–3).

The word for *ministered* here is the same word used to describe the duties of the Levites in the Old Testament. This verse paints a picture of these ministers praising and worshipping God. From it, we can see that this was a special time of praise and worship because they were fasting. They must have sensed that God wanted to do something or say something, so they set food aside and took that time to praise, worship, and wait on God.

How many things have we missed in our lives because we have ignored the small promptings of the Spirit of God? We sensed He wanted to do something, but we rushed past His leading and did not take time to wait on Him in our individual lives or during corporate gatherings of worship. I am sure we have all done that at some point in our lives. Yet, the more we follow the leading of God and spend time waiting on God, the richer and more effective our lives will become.

> How many things have we missed in our lives because we have ignored the small promptings of the Spirit of God?

As these ministers waited on God, the Holy Spirit spoke to them through one or more of the vocal gifts of the Spirit. We will examine these gifts later in this book, but for clarity, the vocal gifts of the Spirit are prophecy, different kinds of tongues, and the interpretation of tongues. After the ministers heard the direction of the Holy Spirit, they spent even more time waiting on God in prayer and fasting. At the conclusion of this time, they prayed and laid their hands on Paul and Barnabas, and God launched them into the ministry He had prepared for them. The next verse,

Acts 13:4, has been an important Scripture in my life: "So, being sent out by the Holy Spirit, they went down to Seleucia, and from there they sailed to Cyprus" (Acts 13:4).

Years ago, when I was in senior year in high school, Pastor Mark Hankins was preaching at my home church's annual convention. I was in my last week of high school; in addition to the excitement of graduation, I was experiencing supernatural encounters from God during this convention. I remember when Pastor Hankins prayed and laid his hands on me. For the rest of the week, I felt aware of the presence of God; it literally felt like a hand was still on my forehead. Beyond the supernatural sign and wonder I was experiencing, a message Pastor Hankins spoke impacted me even more powerfully. Since I had an exam, I wasn't able to attend this service in person, so I listened to the message on CD. In that message, he shared about being "Sent forth by the Holy Ghost." I listened to that message over and over again. During the next year, I would often set my alarm clock stereo to wake me up to that message. Whenever I was facing a struggle, I would turn on that message. It would strengthen me and give me hope, because I knew God had sent me.

It is important that you know that God has sent you. Because whoever sends you has to back you. Too many people make important life decisions based on the opinions of others. Others may be well intentioned, but when it comes down to it, you must know God has sent you, because if He sent you, you know He can provide for you like no other person can. If you know God has sent you, you know your struggle has purpose. You know your struggle is not your end, but that a great victory exists on the other side of the struggle. When you know God has sent you, you can have hope and the courage of a superhero during the storm, because your confidence is in God.

Paul and Barnabas were launched into the next phase of their lives because they waited on God. Instead of skipping by the leading of the Lord, they waited on Him and received direction and launching into the next phase of their lives. Kenneth E. Hagin, the man of God who trained my pastor who trained me, would talk about phases in life and ministry. He once said that many people live and die and never get into phase one of what God has called them to do.

Your hunger for God will open doors for you to encounter Him and experience the best of life that He has for you.

How many times do we miss directions and doorways in our purpose because we do not take time to wait on God? How many times have we missed opportunities to have superhuman results because we did not take the time to wait on Him? Let your hunger for the Lord motivate you and drive you to wait on Him. Your hunger for God will open doors for you to encounter Him and experience the best of life that He has for you. Hunger after God, wait on Him, and expect wonderful results!

REVERENCE

Fear of the Lord leads to life, and he who has it will abide in satisfaction; he will not be visited with evil (PROVERBS 19:23).

D avid—a warrior king, a skillful psalmist, a famed giant-slayer, a man after God's own heart. Many titles can be applied to this celebrated hero of faith, including, as I shared in the last chapter, a man hungry for God, His presence, and His glory. David's hunger for God even influenced his policies as king. As soon as David became king over all of Israel, one of his first acts was transferring the Ark of the Covenant to Jerusalem.

The Ark of the Covenant was holy to the people of God. This famed ark that we see represented in the movie *Raiders of the Lost Ark* contained the presence of God. At the entrance of the tent of meeting, where the ark resided, the pillar of fire and cloud would hover and appear when Moses met with God. In Exodus 25, God gave specific instructions to Moses concerning the creation and the care of the ark:

Have the people make an Ark of acacia wood—a sacred chest 45 inches long, 27 inches wide, and 27 inches high. Overlay it inside and outside with pure gold, and run a molding of gold all around it. Cast four gold rings and attach them to its four feet, two rings on each side. Make poles from acacia wood, and overlay them with gold. Insert the poles into the rings at the sides of the Ark to carry it. These carrying poles must stay inside the rings; never remove them. When the Ark is finished, place inside it the stone tablets inscribed with the terms of the covenant, which I will give to you. Then make the Ark's cover—the place of atonement—from pure gold. It must be 45 inches long and 27 inches wide. Then make two cherubim from hammered gold, and place them on the two ends of the atonement cover. Mold the cherubim on each end of the atonement cover, making it all of one piece of gold. The cherubim will face each other and look down on the atonement cover. With their wings spread above it, they will protect it. Place inside the Ark the stone tablets inscribed with the terms of the covenant, which I will give to you. Then put the atonement cover on top of the Ark. I will meet with you there and talk to you from above the atonement cover between the gold cherubim that hover over the Ark of the Covenant. From there I will give you my commands for the people of Israel (Exodus 25:10–22 NLT).

As mentioned in the last section, Exodus 33:9 tells us that God spoke to Moses face to face, as a man speaks to his friend. Numbers 7:89 reiterates this when it says:

Whenever Moses went into the Tabernacle to speak with the Lord, he heard the voice speaking to him from between the two cherubim above the Ark's cover— the place of atonement—that rests on the Ark of the Covenant. The Lord spoke to him from there (NLT).

At this holy ark, Moses would intimately meet with God.

In the days of Moses, the Ark of the Covenant went before the people of God as they traveled through the wilderness. In the days of Joshua's leadership, the River Jordan parted like the Red Sea before the ark and those who carried it. In the days of Samuel's youth, Samuel heard God's voice as he slept near the ark. This ark held a unique place in the history of the people of God, and later generations would call it the ark of God's strength or the symbol of God's power (see Ps. 132:8 KJV, NLT). From the days of Samuel to the days of Isaiah, they rightly spoke of God dwelling between the cherubim, which is a reference to God's manifest presence being upon the Ark of the Covenant. The ark housed the manifest presence of God, the tablets of the covenant, Aaron's staff that had budded, and manna from the wilderness. It is no wonder David wanted the ark near him. He was a man hungry for God, His presence, and His glory.

The day finally arrived for David and Israel to move the ark to Jerusalem. Imagine the excitement flooding David's being. He was king, and now he was about realize a dream come true, moving the ark to Jerusalem. Second Samuel 6 tells us that David gathered thirty thousand elite troops and led them to bring the ark to Jerusalem. They placed the Ark of the Covenant on a new cart. Uzzah and Ahio, members of the house that were guarding the ark, guided the ark toward its destination. David and all the people of Israel were celebrating, playing instruments, and singing as they accompanied the ark to Jerusalem.

Why did divine judgment interrupt this joyous day? Why did divine judgment bring David's parade to a halt? It happened because of Uzzah's lack of respect or reverence.

It was a joyous day and a grand parade. It was a day to be celebrated. Everything *seemed* like it was going extremely well until they arrived at the threshing floor of Nacon. At the threshing floor of Nacon, the oxen who were pulling the cart that carried the ark stumbled. Uzzah instinctively reached out his hand to steady the ark. As soon as he touched it, he died.

> *But when they came to Nacon's threshing floor, the oxen stumbled. So Uzzah reached out for the ark of God and grabbed it. The Lord became angry with Uzzah, so God killed him there for his lack of respect. He died beside the ark of God* (2 Samuel 6:6–7 GW).

The Hebrew words describing anger in this verse point to wrath, which is a form of divine judgment. Why did divine judgment interrupt this joyous day? Why did divine judgment bring David's parade to a halt? It happened because of Uzzah's lack of respect or reverence. Lack of respect toward the Ark of the Covenant had brought disaster in prior years; the Philistines and the people at Beth-shemesh experienced the disaster firsthand (see 1 Sam. 6).

> Uzzah's lack of respect did not begin with grabbing the holy ark; it began with placing the ark on the cart.

The house of Abinadab, father to Uzzah and Ahio, was chosen to be the guardian of the ark, because he and his family understood how to care for it. The ark stayed with their family for decades without any negative instances.

Uzzah's lack of respect did not begin with grabbing the holy ark; it began with placing the ark on the cart. Look again at what God said to Moses:

> *Cast four gold rings and attach them to its four feet, two rings on each side. Make poles from acacia wood, and overlay them with gold. Insert the poles into the rings at the sides of the Ark to carry it. These carrying poles must stay inside the rings; never remove them* (Exodus 25:12–15 NLT).

In Numbers 4, God gave even more specific instructions on how to transport the Ark of the Covenant. In these step-by-step details, God said the ark and other holy objects should be covered with multiple layers of certain fabrics. After the ark was covered, the ark should be transported by four priests carrying the ark by its poles. The lack of reverence and respect in Uzzah was displayed in his complete disregard for the proper method of handling the ark. If the ark had been carried by priests, it would not have stumbled. If the ark was covered, it could not be grabbed.

The idea of placing the Ark of the Covenant on a cart came from the Philistines. The Philistines placed the Ark of the Covenant on a cart to send it away from their territories (see 1 Sam. 6). Never let those who oppose God set the standard of how the people of God should treat God. Yet, this is what Uzzah, David, and the rest of Israel did. They went against God's instructions and, in doing so, displayed their lack of respect and reverence for God, His word, and His ways.

After the outbreak of divine judgment, the party was over. The singing stopped; the celebration and parade came to a screeching halt. David was angry, upset, and afraid. He left the ark in the house of Obed-edom, headed back to Jerusalem, and wondered how he would ever transport the ark to be near him.

It took more than three months for David to return for the ark. During those three months, the ark did not sit dormant. The power and blessing of God flowed from the ark, affecting Obed-edom, his house, all those who lived there, all of his livestock, and all of his property. The monumental level of blessing that Obed-edom experienced was so immense that reports of the blessing reached King David. "Then King David was told, 'The Lord has blessed Obed-edom's household and everything he has because of the Ark of God'" (2 Samuel 6:12 NLT).

After hearing these reports, David returned to his goal of bringing the Ark of the Covenant to Jerusalem. However, this time he changed his methodology. King David still brought the ark to Jerusalem with a great celebration of singing and music, but this time he followed the Lord's instructions regarding the transportation of the ark. In addition, every time those who were carrying the ark traveled six steps, David worshipped God through offering sacrifices. On top of the singing, music, celebrating, and worship,

David also danced before God with all of his might. This was not a quick procession.

This celebratory transfer of the ark took time and was overflowing with reverence, worship, and praise to God. This parade from the house of Obed-edom to Jerusalem showcased David's hunger and reverence. The Ark of the Covenant arrived in Jerusalem, and eventually, under King Solomon, it moved to the temple that God had commissioned Solomon to build.

> Hunger is not enough; we also need reverence. That is why I say that the adventure of flowing in the Spirit begins at the crossroads of hunger and reverence.

We are under a new covenant as New Testament believers. According to the New Testament, we handle holy things on a regular basis that used to be reserved only for priests and those in special categories. Under this new covenant, we could enter the Holy of Holies and not perish because of the shed blood of Jesus. Even in our error, we would not have the same results as Uzzah and others because of our new covenant and the shedding of Jesus' blood. Although all of this is true, we must learn from this example of the importance of reverence. Hunger is not enough; we also need reverence. That is why I say that the adventure of flowing in the Spirit begins at the crossroads of hunger *and* reverence.

The books of Job, Psalms, Proverbs, and Ecclesiastes all share the importance of the fear of the Lord. The fear of the Lord does not mean that you should be afraid of God. *The fear of the Lord* can be defined as "reverential awe and respect toward God and His ways." A person can have the definition of the fear of the Lord and still not understand it. Proverbs 2:5 says, "Then you will understand the fear of the Lord, and find the knowledge of God." The *then* in this verse tells us that the previous verses share insight into the process of understanding the fear of the Lord. Let's look at these four verses one by one.

> The fear of the Lord does not mean that you should be afraid of God.

First, in Proverbs 2:1, it says, "My son, if you receive my words, and treasure my commands within you." The first step in this process of understanding the fear of the Lord is receiving the words of God. Receiving does not mean hearing. *Receive* means "to take it, to grab it, to accept it." Many people hear the word of God and never receive it. Jesus shared about it extensively in Mark 4. In receiving the word, you accept the word as true even if it confronts the way you are currently living. Furthermore, receiving the word means choosing the word over your current circumstances, past experiences, and everything you may have previously thought or learned.

The second step in this process is to treasure the commands or the word of God. Psalm 119:11 says, "Your word I have hidden in my heart, that I might not sin against You." In Matthew 12:35, Jesus referred to the heart as a treasury or a storehouse. You store the Word in your heart by continually reading it, hearing it, and receiving it. You do not arrive at the fear of the Lord just because you received the word one time. You must continually hear, read, and receive the word.

Then, Proverbs 2:2 says, "So that you incline your ear to wisdom, and apply your heart to understanding." The third step in the process of understanding the fear of the Lord is to incline your ear to wisdom. *Incline* means "to hear and be attentive to." To incline your ear means to tune your ear to hear God's wisdom. (I will cover wisdom in detail in a later section of this book.) The inclining of your ear includes an expectation to receive wisdom from God and a conscious decision to turn away from other voices that would dissuade you from following God's ways.

The fourth step of this process is to apply your heart to understanding. *Apply* means "to stretch out, extend, and incline." *Heart* refers to the inner you—your soul and spirit. This verse indicates that the fourth step is directing your heart and mind to understanding and stretching your way of thinking to understand what God's word is saying.

Next, Proverbs 2:3 says, "Yes, if you cry out for discernment [knowledge in the KJV], and lift up your voice for understanding." Crying after and lifting up your voice are two different ways to describe prayer. Knowledge, understanding, and wisdom are often connected in the book of Proverbs. The fourth step in this process is consistently praying, in a heartfelt way, for discernment, knowledge, and understanding.

Lastly, Proverbs 2:4 says, "If you seek her as silver, and search for her as for hidden treasures." The desire for knowledge and understanding cannot stop at prayer. Verse four says we must search for knowledge, understanding, and wisdom in the same way that a treasure hunter would seek for hidden treasure. Our desire should match the intensity, passion, effort, planning, and persistence of a treasure hunter. The fifth step of this process is to hungrily search for God's knowledge, understanding, and wisdom. This search is carried out through reading the scripture, hearing the word taught and preached, and living open to direction and revelation from the Spirit of God.

If you continually receive the word, store up the word in your heart, tune your ear expectantly to hear wisdom, direct your heart toward wisdom, stretch your way of thinking to understand, fervently pray for these things, and search for them with great passion, then you will understand the reverential awe and respect of God. Understanding the fear of the Lord is a process and a lifestyle. Living in the fear of the Lord means continually examining your actions in light of God's word. As you examine your actions, reverence for God becomes a determining factor in your decision-making process.

The lifestyle of reverential awe toward God brings wonderful benefits, such as extended life (see Prov. 10:27) and protection for you and your children (see Prov. 14:26). The fear of the Lord is called a fountain of life (see Prov. 14:27), and it will cause you to live a satisfying life (see Prov. 19:23), protect you from harm (see Prov. 19:23), and bring riches to your life (see Prov. 22:4). Living in reverential awe toward God causes you to experience a superhuman life—a life that is long, satisfying, protected, full of wisdom, and enriched.

As mentioned earlier, the fear of the Lord is not a call to be afraid of God or a list of rules to follow. The fear of the Lord is reverential awe and respect toward God, His word, and His ways. The lack of respect toward God's ways cost Uzzah dearly; our lack of respect under the New Testament causes us to miss out on the wonderful superhuman life that God has destined us to experience.

God has not destined you to live a life that is apart from or that contradicts His word. The superhuman life that God has for you will always be in line with His word. Do not miss out on the superhuman life God has for you because you refuse to receive God's word and respect His ways. The word of God reveals the ways of God. The ways of God often contradict popular philosophies; even still, believers have to respect God's ways enough to choose His ways over the world's ways.

God stated this clearly in Isaiah 55:8–9:

> *"For My thoughts are not your thoughts, nor are your ways My ways," says the Lord. "For as the heavens are higher than the earth, so are My ways higher than your ways, and My thoughts than your thoughts."*

You may wonder, *How can I ever think the thoughts of God or understand the ways of God?* You may think it's impossible. It is not impossible if God is your teacher. If you follow the process to understanding the fear of the Lord, you will begin to understand His ways. In a lifestyle of reverencing God, you must always view God's word and ways as higher, greater, and weightier than your own personal opinion and whatever the world is promoting. As the psalmist declared: "Let all the earth fear the Lord; let all the inhabitants of the world stand in awe of Him" (Psalm 33:8).

So far, we have defined *fear of the Lord* as respect toward God, His word, and His ways, but another part of the definition of the *fear of the Lord* is reverential awe. Awe means too little to our generation because of how frequently we use the word *awesome*. Everything is awesome. Pizza is awesome. Someone's suit is awesome. A new car is awesome. A vacation is awesome. A new job is awesome. A watch is awesome. A new computer is awesome. The frequency with which we have used *awesome* has altered our understanding of the meaning of the word and has made it a cultural expression. But to be in *awe* in a biblical sense means "to have a feeling of reverential respect mixed with wonder and amazement."

I have seen natural things that have left me standing in awe. When I traveled to Niagara Falls, my family and I took a boat to see the Falls up close. Before our boat ride, we had experienced parts of the Falls. We descended 175 feet in an elevator and walked out a tunnel to see the rushing water. When I looked to the left, I could see parts of the Horseshoe Falls, and when I looked to the right, I could see parts of the American Falls and the Bridal Veil Falls. We took the path that led us to the base of a portion of the Bridal Veil Falls. As we climbed the stairs, we reached a place where we could stand under the Falls and experience its force. The entire time, from when I walked out of the tunnel until I stood under the Falls, was an amazing experience.

After this experience, my wife and I wondered if the boat ride would be worth it. Our boat passed the American Falls and the Bridal Veil Falls, and we were able to fully see these Falls from another view. We took pictures and recorded videos with the rest of the tourists on the boat. Our boat continued down the river, and moments later we could see the Horseshoe Falls. As the water rushed down the Falls, creating a massive mist, a complete rainbow appeared in the midst of it. I stopped recording with my cell phone, took in the sight, and whispered, "Whoa." I was in awe. I was standing in awe of God's majestic creation. When is the last time you said *whoa* or *wow* in response to God?

The psalmist declared in Psalm 33:8 that the whole world should reverence God and that everyone should stand in awe of Him. Many believers reverence God, but have forgotten their awe. Often, we rightfully think of and refer to God as our heavenly Father. We rightfully consider Him our friend and the one who loves us in a way that surpasses knowledge. He is all of those things to us, but He is also an awesome God. As Psalm 77:14 declares, "You are the God of great wonders! You demonstrate your awesome power among the nations" (NLT).

Many believers reverence God, but have forgotten their awe.

Our God is an awesome God, and He performs great wonders. *Wonders* are "marvels, extraordinary things, and events that cause admiration and amazement." To *wonder* is "to experience a feeling of surprise mixed with admiration caused by something beautiful, unexpected, unfamiliar, or inexplicable." How often have you experienced this side of God? No matter how often you have experienced this side of Him, God wants you to experience even more. The secret to experiencing more of this side of God is to avoid becoming overfamiliar. Experiencing this side of God should be our normal, but we must not become overfamiliar with it. When people are overfamiliar with anything, they tend to consider that thing and speak of that thing in an inappropriately informal way. Overfamiliarity leads to devaluing, which can border on ingratitude and unappreciation.

Many believers are mature and respectful, but they have lost or are losing their awe of God because of their indifference to the things of God. These believers sometimes compare what they see to previous moves of God, and they lose their sense of awe in the comparison. If our response to a message is, "Well, I've heard that before," and our response to a miracle is, "Well, I've seen that before," we are causing ourselves to miss the wonderful things that God wants to reveal to us. You may be a believer who has experienced awesome and wonderful things in God, but I beg you, please do not allow comparison to steal your sense of awe. Be amazed by the "small things" as well as the "big things."

> The secret to experiencing more of this side of God is to avoid becoming overfamiliar.

If you have ever have been in the presence of a small child at a theme park or a zoo, you know that everything amazes them. Everything is, "Dad, wow, look at that!" "Mom, look! Look! That is so cool." What is coming from the small child is not just a cultural expression, but a genuine expression of amazement, wonder, and awe. The child will have a wonderful experience at that place because of his or her outlook. If you have lost your awe or just want to experience more of this side of God, start being amazed at the "small things" and the things you have heard and experienced before. As you make the decision to be amazed and grateful at everything God does, you will position yourself to experience wonders from God that will make you say, *Whoa!* In addition to positioning yourself to experience wonders, you will also position yourself to be used by God to do superhuman things that cause those who see you to stand in awe of your God.

We have finally arrived at the crossroads of hunger and reverence. Let's begin our journey into the superhuman life that reaches beyond mere human limitations. As I will share in the next section, God has already made you more than realize you are.

SECRET 3

NEW CREATION REALITIES

Therefore, if anyone is in Christ, he is a new creation; old things have passed away; behold, all things have become new (2 CORINTHIANS 5:17).

Peter Parker was an ordinary teenager. If you saw him, you would probably describe him as an average teenager. If you got to know him, you might describe him as smart, nerdy, and interested in science. He was a normal teenager when he went on a field trip to a laboratory. Unbeknownst to him, a radioactive spider had escaped its cage and crawled on him. Peter cried out in pain and knocked the bug away. Aside from the stinging of the bite, Peter did not think anything had changed. He thought he was still an ordinary teenager. Yet, when he was bitten by the radioactive spider, he received superhuman abilities that set him on the path to becoming *Spider-man*. He did not know it yet, but he was no longer a mere mortal.

Bruce Banner was a brilliant, mild-mannered scientist. During the experimental testing of a gamma bomb, Bruce was exposed to dangerously high levels of gamma radiation. The exposure changed everything. He was no longer a mere mortal; he was *The Hulk.*

Reed Richards created a spaceship that was able to travel into deep space. He, his girlfriend Susan Storm, his girlfriend's brother Johnny Storm, and his best friend Ben Grimm set out on their exploration of space. While in space, the four encountered a cosmic storm that released powerful levels of radiation. When they returned to earth, they realized they were different. Their molecules had been altered. They were no longer mere mortals, and they would become known as *The Fantastic Four.*

Barry Allen was working late one night in a police laboratory. While working, Barry was struck by lightning, which caused nearby chemicals to spill and cover him. Barry Allen was no longer a mere mortal; he was now the world's fastest man, *The Flash.*

Peter, Bruce, Reed, Susan, Johnny, Ben, and Barry were all mere mortals until an incident changed their lives forever. This incident, whether caused by chemicals, lightning, or radiation, altered their beings and gave them superhuman abilities. Similarly, every believer has had an incident that has altered their being and granted them superhuman abilities. We call that incident being *born again.*

Peter the apostle described it this way: "Having been born again, not of corruptible seed but incorruptible, through the word of God which lives and abides forever" (1 Peter 1:23). The phrase *born again* or *begotten us again* (see 1 Pet. 1:3) means "to be born anew, to produce again, and to be regenerated." When a living organism regenerates, it regrows new tissue to replace lost or injured tissues. When people are born again, their spirits are regenerated.

The incorruptible seed of the word of God is the source tissue for the regeneration of the believer. Every believer is born again of the incorruptible seed of the word of God, which means no believers are born again out of a lesser material. The spiritual DNA of every believer comes from the word of God. When a believer is born again, the believer is regrown into a new creation that has never been seen before. Once born again, a person is no longer a mere mortal.

Jesus explained this to the Pharisee Nicodemus:

> *Jesus answered and said to him, "Most assuredly, I say to you, unless one is born again, he cannot see the kingdom of God."*
>
> *Nicodemus said to Him, "How can a man be born when he is old? Can he enter a second time into his mother's womb and be born?"*
>
> *Jesus answered, "Most assuredly, I say to you, unless one is born of water and the Spirit, he cannot enter the kingdom of God. That which is born of the flesh*

is flesh, and that which is born of the Spirit is spirit. Do not marvel that I said to you, 'You must be born again'" (John 3:3–7).

When speaking to Nicodemus, Jesus used *born again* to mean "born from above, born from a higher place, born over again." The second birth Jesus referred to is spiritual. This birth is produced by the Spirit of God and is of heavenly origin.

Every Christmas, believers all around the world celebrate that Jesus came from heaven and was born of a virgin. To say that Jesus is not of this world or from this world is not a shocking statement to any believer. He's from heaven, and so are you. When you were born again, born from above, you were given a new origin story. Many people are familiar with Superman's origin story—that he came from the planet Krypton. Heaven is now part of every believer's origin story. No matter where the person was when they accepted Jesus as their Lord and Savior, they were born from heaven above.

Heaven is now part of
every believer's origin story.

The apostle John said it this way: "Beloved, let us love one another, for love is of God; and everyone who loves is born of God and knows God" (1 John 4:7). When John talked about the new birth, he called it being "born of God." The DNA of the incorruptible seed of the word of God in your spirit came straight from God Himself. You have been born again; you are no longer a mere mortal. One of the worst things you can do after you are born again is to consider yourself "only human" and just a mere mortal. You are not just human. You are not a mere mortal. The new birth granted you a new spiritual DNA, a new origin story, and a brand-new identity as a new creation in Christ Jesus.

Similarly, Paul said, "Therefore, if anyone is in Christ, he is a new creation; old things have passed away; behold, all things have become new" (2 Corinthians 5:17). When Paul spoke of the new birth, he referred to believers as new creatures or new creations. A new creature is a brand-new being that has never been seen before. This new creature has a different nature than the creature it replaced. The new creature has abilities that the old creature did not possess. The new creature has an identity that the old creature could not fathom. The new creature has rights that the old creature could not claim. The new creature has power with God and power over the enemy. The new creature has a vastly different reality than the old creature.

> Many believers never experience the superhuman life because they fail to grasp new creation realities.

Many believers never experience the superhuman life because they fail to grasp new creation realities. Instead of clinging to the new, they embrace the old. If people desire to understand who they are as new creatures in Christ Jesus, they must renovate their minds to the truth of what God's word says about them. As Paul said, in Romans 12:2:

> *And do not be conformed to this world, but be transformed by the renewing of your mind, that you may prove what is that good and acceptable and perfect will of God.*
>
> *Don't copy the behavior and customs of this world, but let God transform you into a new person by changing the way you think. Then you will learn to know God's will for you, which is good and pleasing and perfect* (NLT).

If people are born again, yet never change the way they think, they will still act like they are not born again. When the Scripture says that all things have become new, it is referring to the spirit of the person. The spirit has been regenerated, the mind has not. In order to experience new creation realities, the spirit must be regenerated and the mind must be renovated. When you renovate a room, you take out the old and replace it with the new. When you renovate your mind, you take out the old way of thinking and replace it with a new way of thinking. This new way of thinking should be rooted in the word of God.

> In order to experience new creation realities, the spirit must be regenerated and the mind must be renovated.

The renovation of the mind leads to the transformation of the life. The superhuman effects of regeneration in the life of a believer is limited by the extent to which the mind has been renovated. It is simple: If you do not renew your mind, you will not enjoy the superhuman life that God has for you. The word for *transform* in Romans 12:2 illustrates a beautiful and powerful example. *Transform* means "to change into another form and to transfigure." In Romans 12:2, it says we are transformed by the renewing of our minds. The fact that the word is *renewing* instead of *renewed* tells us that this is a continual process, not a one-time event. The renewing of the mind is a process that begins at salvation and continues throughout the Christian life.

Many believers are saved, but they do not live like it because of their thinking. As I mentioned before, when we are born again, our spirits are saved. Even though are spirits are saved, we will live like we are not saved if we do not renew our minds to the truth of God's word. Many Christians have renewed their minds concerning right and wrong, holiness and wickedness, the fruit of the Spirit and the works of the flesh. All of those things are vital, and believers must continually renew their minds on those subjects; however, those are not the only topics on which believers must renew their minds. If believers do not renew their minds concerning their identity as new creations in Christ Jesus, they will not experience the superhuman life that Jesus made available for them.

Romans 12:2 tells us that we are transformed by the renewing of our minds. Our spirits are regenerated and transformed when we are born again. Our lives are transformed through the renewing of our minds. The Greek word for *transformed* in Romans 12:2 is very interesting, since it is only used three other times in the New Testament. Two of those three times refer to what many believers call The Transfiguration:

> *Now after six days Jesus took Peter, James, and John his brother, led them up on a high mountain by themselves, and He was transfigured before them. His face shone like the sun, and his clothes became as white as the light* (Matthew 17:1–2).
>
> *Now after six days Jesus took Peter, James, and John, and led them up on a high mountain apart by themselves; and He was transfigured before them. His clothes became shining, exceedingly white, like snow, such as no launderer on earth can whiten them* (Mark 9:2–3).

Imagine how extreme Jesus' transformation must have seemed to Peter, James, and John. They were walking together, and Jesus looked the same way He did the entire three years they had known Him. The four were conversing as they traveled up the mountain. Jesus began to pray, and the three disciples watched. The gospels note on different occasions how the disciples would watch Jesus pray and learn from His example. During this time of prayer, the three apostles observed something vastly different. As Jesus prayed, His face began to shine like the sun. His clothes suddenly changed and became as white as the light. The power that radiated from Jesus was so strong that it knocked the three disciples from their feet and caused them to lose consciousness.

Everything about this time with Jesus seemed ordinary to them until Jesus was transformed in front of them and, as the Amplified Bible Classic Edition says, "He was transfigured before them and became resplendent with divine brightness." Jesus' transfiguration on the mount was a transformation. What a transformation! The transformation of a person into a new creation is just as awe-inspiring. What God does in believers the moment they are born again is even more amazing than the transfiguration of Jesus upon the mountain. Jesus was transfigured to reveal who He really was; we are transformed to reveal who He has re-created us to be.

The third place the Greek word for *transformed* is used is in 2 Corinthians 3:18, which says:

> *But we all, with unveiled face, beholding as in a mirror the glory of the Lord, are being transformed*

into the same image from glory to glory, just as by the Spirit of the Lord.

Just as in Romans 12, this verse speaks of the transformation of the life of the believer. The latter part of this verse in the New Living Translation says, "And the Lord—who is the Spirit—makes us more and more like him as we are changed into his glorious image." Our lives are transformed into the superhuman life as we renew our minds with the new creation realities found in the word of God. The sad truth is that believers will never realize what God has accomplished in them until they renovate their minds to new creation realities.

> Our lives are transformed into the superhuman life as we renew our minds with the new creation realities found in the word of God.

In this chapter so far, we have examined the importance of renovating our minds concerning new creation realities. Now, let's look specifically at the new creation realities we must embrace.

1. It's Already Done.

You are not becoming a new creature; if you have been born again, you are already a new creature. It is highly frustrating trying to become something you already are. The first new creation reality you must embrace is that *you are a new creature.* The Scripture is very clear concerning that: "Therefore, if anyone is in Christ, he is a new creation; old things have passed away; behold, all things have become new" (2 Corinthians 5:17). Stop trying to become a new creature and accept the reality that you already are one.

2. You Are Not an Old Sinner Saved by Grace.

But God is so rich in mercy, and he loved us so much, that even though we were dead because of our sins, he gave us life when he raised Christ from the dead. (It is only by God's grace that you have been saved!) (Ephesians 2:4–5 NLT).

You are not an old sinner saved by grace! That is an oxymoron. You are either an old sinner *or* you are saved by grace. When you were born again, your identity changed. You are no longer a sinner; you may sin, but you are not a sinner. Sinning after salvation does not change your identity back to being a sinner. Stop identifying as a sinner and embrace the reality of the gift of being saved by grace.

3. You Are the Righteousness of God in Christ Jesus.

Paul wrote, "For He made Him who knew no sin to be sin for us, that we might become the righteousness of God in Him" (2 Corinthians 5:21). You are not an old sinner; you are the righteousness of God in Christ Jesus. *Righteousness* is the state that is acceptable to God; it simply means "to be in right standing with God." Righteousness is the standing of every believer. In a courtroom, everyone does not have standing. Only those who have standing can bring a lawsuit in the court. Every believer has standing with God and has the right to "boldly approach the throne of grace" to receive grace, mercy, and help in their time of need (Hebrews 4:16). Your sin does not change your standing; if your sin changed your standing, you would not be able to go to the throne of grace.

> You are not an old sinner; you are the righteousness of God in Christ Jesus.

Think about it this way: Before you were born again, you did good things. Yet none of the good deeds you accomplished made you righteous. You became righteous when you believed in Jesus (see Rom. 3:22). You did not become righteous because you kept a list of commandments. You became righteous because you put your faith in Jesus. In the same way that doing something good did not make you righteous, sinning does not make you unrighteous. However, this is not a license to sin. Our standing is righteousness, and our conduct should be holiness.

4. You Are Forgiven.

Believers have been forgiven, and the blood of Jesus has washed away all of their sins. The Bible clearly establishes this:

> *And from Jesus Christ, the faithful witness, the first-born from the dead, and the ruler over the kings of the earth. To Him who loved us and washed us from our sins in His own blood* (Revelation 1:5).
>
> *You were dead because of your sins and because your sinful nature was not yet cut away. Then God made you alive with Christ, for he forgave all our sins* (Colossians 2:13 NLT).

To experience the superhuman life and live in new creation realities, you must believe you are forgiven. You may think that seems elementary and basic, but many people deeply struggle within their hearts to believe God has forgiven them for certain actions, mistakes, and sins. The price Jesus paid on the cross handled our past and any sins we may commit in the future.

To experience the superhuman life and live in new creation realities, you must believe you are forgiven.

What should believers do if they sin? In 1 John 1:9, it says, "If we confess our sins, He is faithful and just to forgive us our sins and to cleanse us from all unrighteousness." The only thing left after God forgives your sin and cleanses you from all unrighteousness is *righteousness*. You are not your sin. You are not a sinner. You are forgiven, and you are the righteousness of God in Christ Jesus. If you believe you are a sinner and focus on sin, you will become sin conscious and continue in sin. Sin consciousness will prevent you from experiencing new creation realities. Instead of focusing on sin, focus on righteousness and the truth that you are a new creation in Christ Jesus.

5. You Have Divine Access.

As you understand you are forgiven and have been made righteous, you will then realize that nothing stands between you and God. As it says in Hebrews:

> *And so, dear brothers and sisters, we can boldly enter heaven's Most Holy Place because of the blood of Jesus. By his death, Jesus opened a new and life-giving way through the curtain into the Most Holy Place* (Hebrews 10:19–20 NLT).

Some believers erroneously believe that when they sin, they should pull away from God in fear that He is angry at them. Other believers will not bring certain situations to God because they think such things are not big enough or spiritual enough to warrant His attention. The truth is,

God wants to hear from you. Jesus paid a great price so that you can come boldly to the throne of God at any time for any reason. If you sin, do not run from God. Run to Him! If you have a small concern or request, bring it to Him. If you do not think it is spiritual enough, bring it to Him. If you just want to spend time with Him, come to Him. As a new creation, you have been given divine access to the throne of God. You belong there with your heavenly Father.

6. You Are Redeemed.

Christ has redeemed us from the curse of the law, having become a curse for us (for it is written, "Cursed is everyone who hangs on a tree" (Galatians 3:13).

Knowing that you were not redeemed with corruptible things, like silver or gold, from your aimless conduct received by tradition from your fathers, but with the precious blood of Christ, as of a lamb without blemish and without spot (1 Peter 1:18–19).

To be *redeemed* is "to be bought back, to be liberated due to the payment of a ransom, and to be delivered." Redemption pictures believers as being redeemed from the slave market of sin. Previously, Satan held them captive in sin, darkness, evil, and despair. When they were born again, they were ransomed and walked out of the slavery of sin. When they were redeemed from sin, they were also redeemed from several other things.

> Believers put up with many things
> in their lives that they have actually
> been redeemed and delivered from.

Believers put up with many things in their lives that they have actually been redeemed and delivered from. Galatians 3 declares that believers are redeemed from the curse of the law. The curse of the law is detailed in Deuteronomy 28. In summary, the curse of the law is sickness, poverty, defeat, destruction, family and relationship trauma, poor mental health, and premature death. If you know you are redeemed, when these things show up in your life, you will fight them instead of accepting them. Don't accept everything that shows up. Resist the curse and obey Psalm 107:2 instead, which says, "Let the redeemed of the Lord say so, whom He has redeemed from the hand of the enemy."

7. You Have the Advantage.

The apostle Paul said, "For in Christ Jesus neither circumcision nor uncircumcision avails anything, but a new creation" (Galatians 6:15). The word *avails* means "to have the advantage or to have a condition or circumstance that causes a person to be in a favorable or superior position." In this Scripture, Paul made it clear that in Christ circumcision or uncircumcision do not give believers an advantage in this life. What gives you the advantage is being a new creature, a new creation. When you were born again, you were given the advantage in life.

You are not at a disadvantage. Others may have more privilege than you in certain areas, but you are not at a disadvantage. Do not let any person or group cause you to believe you are disadvantaged. You have the advantage. The new creation has put you in the condition that causes you to always be in a favorable and superior position.

8. You Are an Overcomer.

For whatsoever is born of God overcomes the world. And this is the victory that has overcome the world— our faith. Who is he who overcomes the world, but he who believes that Jesus is the Son of God? (1 John 5:4–5).

God has not planned a life of defeat for you. You were born again to win. In this life, you will face difficulty and various attacks of the enemy. Do not let the difficulties of life and the attacks of demonic forces dishearten you, cause you to despair, or persuade you to quit. Instead of giving up, you must embrace the new creation reality that you are an overcomer. An overcomer does not only win; an overcomer overwhelms, overpowers, vanquishes, and conquers the opposing force. Never forget what Romans 8:38 says about you—that you are more than a conqueror through Him who loves you! As a new creation, you are not fighting for victory; you are fighting from a place of victory. You are already on the winning side, so gives thanks to God who always causes you to triumph (see 2 Cor. 2:14).

> An overcomer does not only win; an overcomer overwhelms, overpowers, vanquishes, and conquers the opposing force.

9. You Have a New Nature.

The new creation comes with a new nature. The apostle Peter explained it this way:

As His divine power has given to us all things that pertain to life and godliness, through the knowledge of Him who called us by glory and virtue, by which have been given to us exceedingly great and precious promises, that through these you may be partakers of the divine nature, having escaped the corruption that is in the world through lust (2 Peter 1:3–4).

Nature refers to "physical origin and innate properties and powers that differ from one person to another." In our new nature, believers receive divine innate properties and powers. These properties and powers enable believers to escape the corruption, destruction, and perishing that is in the world. All believers can access the divine properties and powers within them by faith in God's wonderful promises.

The divine nature is the nature of God. The nature of God allows believers to experience life as God has it and live the way He has instructed us to live. The nature of God is filled with power, glory, abilities, and the fruit of the Spirit (see Gal. 5:22–23).

10. Your Limits Have Been Removed.

Likewise the Spirit also helps in our weaknesses. For we do not know what we should pray for as we ought, but the Spirit Himself makes intercession for us with groanings which cannot be uttered (Romans 8:26).

Weaknesses can also refer to our limitations. The Greek word for *help* describes "working with others to help them obtain something." This word also means "to take hold of an object with another." The Holy Spirit will help you take hold of your weaknesses by strengthening you and enlightening you to help you overcome them. The Holy Spirit also works with you to take you past your limitations. The Holy Spirit causes believers to experience the limitless life of new creation realities. God is not limiting you; often, people limit what God can do in their lives (see Ps. 78:41). Thinking with a non-renovated mind will cause you to live limited. Fitting in with the world and forsaking the reverential awe of God will cause you to live limited. Settling instead of hungering after God will cause you to live limited. As a new creation, your limits have been removed, and God desires to move in your life in ways that are far above everything you can think of, pray for, and imagine (see Eph. 3:20).

> As a new creation, your limits have been removed, and God desires to move in your life in ways that are far above everything you can think of, pray for, and imagine.

11. You Are an Ambassador.

Now then, we are ambassadors for Christ, as though God were pleading through us: we implore you on Christ's behalf, be reconciled to God (2 Corinthians 5:20).

When an ambassador is sent to another country, the ambassador is assigned to represent the interests of the nation or kingdom that sent him or her. The ambassador is authorized by that kingdom. If the ambassador has a need, the commissioning kingdom supplies that need. The ambassador is backed by the full force of the commissioning kingdom. In the same way, believers are ambassadors who are backed by the Kingdom of heaven. When believers set out to fulfill God's plan for their lives, they are not alone; they are backed by the full force of the Kingdom of heaven.

12. You Are Royalty.

For if by the one man's offense death reigned through the one, much more those who receive abundance of grace and of the gift of righteousness will reign in life through the One, Jesus Christ (Romans 5:17).

And has made us kings and priests to His God and Father, to Him be glory and dominion forever and ever. Amen (Revelation 1:6).

As soon as you were born again, you were brought into the royal family of God. You are royalty. Royalty is more than a title or rank; royalty comes with the understanding of certain responsibilities, authority, and protocols. Since believers are royalty, they are not supposed to let life happen to them. Instead, believers are supposed to reign in life. Royalty is the status given to those who are born again; this includes expectations for how they should behave, think, and carry themselves as members of God's royal family.

13. You Are the Temple of God.

Or do you not know that your body is the temple of the Holy Spirit who is in you, whom you have from God, and you are not your own? For you were bought at a price; therefore glorify God in your body and in your spirit, which are God's (1 Corinthians 6:19–20).

One of the marvelous benefits of the new covenant over the old covenant is that believers are the temple of

God. In the Old Testament, the Spirit of God would only rest upon prophets, priests, kings, and certain others with special assignments. No one in the Old Testament had the privilege of being the temple of God. Now, when people are born again, the blood of Jesus cleanses them so well that they become a suitable home to be indwelt by God Himself.

14. You Have a Purpose.

The apostle Paul tells us, "For we are God's masterpiece. He has created us anew in Christ Jesus, so we can do the good things he planned for us long ago" (Ephesians 2:10 NLT). You are not an accident. Your life matters. You have a divine assignment, a calling, and a heavenly purpose. When people think their lives do not matter, they live aimlessly. The purpose God has for you is so grand that it requires you to stop living as a mere mortal. In order to accomplish what God has for you and fulfill your purpose, you must live as a superhuman who understands that you are a new creation in Christ Jesus.

You are not an accident. Your life matters. You have a divine assignment, a calling, and a heavenly purpose.

15. You Are Anointed.

Christ is not Jesus' last name. Christ describes who Jesus is. The word *Christ* means "the Anointed One," and it refers to the anointing Jesus is anointed with. Paul wrote, "Now you are the body of Christ and members individually" (1 Corinthians 12:27). In other words, every believer is part of the body of Christ, meaning every believer is part of the body of the Anointed One. Jesus, the head of the body, is anointed, and so is His body. Every part of the body has been anointed by God to carry out a particular assignment and fulfill a purpose. When the anointing of the Spirit is applied to an individual, it brings unique and powerful abilities that set that person apart from other mortals. The anointing makes all the difference, and God has anointed you!

16. You Are a Spirit.

Now may the God of peace make you holy in every way, and may your whole spirit and soul and body be kept blameless until our Lord Jesus Christ comes again (1 Thessalonians 5:23 NLT).

God has made humans tri-part beings. Many people consider themselves their bodies. Many may consider themselves a combination of their minds and their bodies, but the Scripture reveals the true human creation. Humans are spirits who possess souls and live in physical bodies. You are not your body. Your body is the house you live in. The apostle Peter referred to it as his tabernacle (see 2 Pet. 1:14).

We have the great responsibility of caring for our bodies, because our bodies are the temples of God. Our bodies also give us the right to exist on this planet.

You are not a mind. The soul is the mind, will, and control center of the emotions. You have a soul; but you are not your mind, will, and emotions. You have emotions, but you are not your emotions. People get into trouble when instead of having emotions, they let their emotions have them. The spirit and soul are both eternal and are so very closely intertwined that it takes the word of God to differentiate between the two (see Heb. 4:12).

You are a spirit. In order to experience the fullness of new creation realities, you have to embrace that you are a spirit. Many people give attention to their bodies through nutrition, exercising, clothing, and the like. All of those things are necessary and good. Many people give attention to their souls by ensuring they have good mental health, controlling their emotions, and increasing their understanding through education. All of those things are necessary and good. In understanding everything I have shared in this section, we must ask the question, "How much attention do we give to our spirits?"

As I shared earlier, when people are born again, their spirits are regenerated. Before salvation, the human spirit is spiritually dead and connected to Satan. Ephesians 2:1–5 says,

And you He made alive, who were dead in tres-passes and sins, in which you once walked according

to the course of this world, according to the prince of the power of the air, the spirit who now works in the sons of disobedience, among whom also we all once conducted ourselves in the lusts of our flesh, fulfilling the desires of the flesh and of the mind, and were by nature children of wrath, just as the others. But God, who is rich in mercy, because of His great love with which He loved us, even when we were dead in trespasses, made us alive together with Christ (by grace you have been saved).

When you were born again, your spirit was made alive. Your spirit is no longer connected to Satan, but you are now one spirit with the Lord Jesus (see 1 Cor. 6:17). Since many people have been taught to live as bodies and souls, it is imperative for believers to re-educate themselves in order to live as spirits. As I mentioned before, taking care of our bodies and souls is important, but we must prioritize taking care of our spirits and learning to live out of our spirits.

One way to embrace new creation realities and learn how to live out of your spirit is through the words of your mouth. I have included a new creation reality confession to help you go further on your journey into the superhuman life. Every morning for the next thirty days, I want you to confidently say the confession below aloud.

New Creation Reality Confession

I am a spirit; I have a soul; I live in a physical body.
I am a new creature. Old things have passed away.
I am not an old sinner. I am saved by grace. I am the
righteousness of God in Christ Jesus. I am forgiven.
I have access to God. I am redeemed. I am not dis-
advantaged in this life. I have the advantage. I am
an overcomer. I have the nature of God. My limits
have been removed. I am an ambassador, and I am
backed by the Kingdom of heaven. I am royalty, and
I reign in this life. I am the temple of the almighty
God. The greater one Himself lives on the inside of
me and has made me greater than anything I will
ever face. I am anointed. I have a purpose, and I
will fulfill it!

The more you say these scriptural words, the more you will believe them, and the more you believe them, the more you will experience them. The words you consistently speak will affect the way you think. Many believers have limited their experience as new creations through their unbiblical mindsets steeped in worldly carnality or religious tradition. In order to experience the new creation reality and progress on their journey into the superhuman life, believers must shift their thinking by renewing their minds, changing how they see themselves, and building a new mentality.

> Many believers have limited their experience as new creations through their unbiblical mindsets steeped in worldly carnality or religious tradition.

Spider-man. She-Hulk. Reed Richards. Sue Richards. Captain America. Flash. Captain Marvel. Their powers differ from one another, but one thing all of these heroes have in common is that they are superhuman and consider themselves heroes. In the world of superheroes, depending on the comic, some individuals are referred to as mutants or meta-humans. These mutants or meta-humans have either been born with superhuman powers or had these powers conferred on to them through some set of circumstances. Once their abilities and powers began to manifest, they had to stop considering themselves as mere mortals. If they only considered themselves as mere mortals, they would never achieve the wonderful results that their powers and abilities could produce.

All believers have been transformed into new creatures in Christ Jesus. Sadly, not enough believers think like they are new creations; instead, they consider themselves as only mere mortals due to worldly carnality or unbiblical religious tradition. Many of these believers are only a mindset shift away from experiencing the superhuman life. Are you ready to shift your mindset?

Look at what the apostle Paul said in 2 Corinthians 10:

For though we walk in the flesh, we do not war according to the flesh. For the weapons of our warfare are not carnal but mighty in God for pulling down strongholds, casting down arguments, and every high thing that exalts itself against the knowledge of God, bringing every thought into captivity to the obedience of Christ (2 Corinthians 10:3–5).

Many believers use this passage of Scripture to talk about spiritual warfare. There is nothing wrong with that; this Scripture does apply to spiritual warfare. However, I want focus on the phrase *pulling down strongholds. Pulling down* speaks of demolition. A *stronghold* is a castle, fortress, or anything on which one relies. Seneca, a first-century Roman philosopher, referred to certain persuasive arguments as strongholds. In the context of 2 Corinthians 10:3–5, we can see that it refers to mental strongholds. A stronghold in your mind can be a mentality, a philosophy, or even an identity. It may be an argument for a set course of actions. It is a mental process or philosophy a person relies on, depends upon, trusts in, and has confidence in.

Very often, we focus on the negative side of strongholds and arguments (also defined as reasonings and thoughts). However, based on the definition of *strongholds*, we see that both godly strongholds and ungodly strongholds exist. Pastor Mac Hammond once said, "Your success in this life will depend on the strongholds you build for yourself and occupy."

Renewing your mind to new creation realities is a process of removing your old way of thinking, embracing the biblical way of thinking, and growing in the new creation reality mindset until it becomes a godly stronghold in your life. The words *high thing* in verse five refer to an elevated place or structure. In many battles, victory has been determined by castles, fortresses, or the group who had the high ground. You must progress in the new creation reality mindset until it becomes high ground, a place you will never cede to an inferior way of thinking.

> If you let your feelings determine who you are, you will have a life of instability that never fully ascends to the heights of what Jesus purchased for you.

"But, I don't feel like a new creation. I feel like an old sinner," you might say. Our feelings do not dictate our reality. If you let your feelings determine who you are, you will have a life of instability that never fully ascends to the heights of what Jesus purchased for you. You must embrace something that is higher than your feelings, which is faith in what God's word says about you.

SECRET 4

FAITH

Now the just shall live by faith; but if anyone draws back, My soul has no pleasure in him (HEBREWS 10:38).

*F**aith* is defined as "firm belief, confidence, assurance, firm persuasion, the conviction of the truth of anything, belief with the predominate idea of trust." Faith is mentioned 245 times in the New Testament, which should be a great insight into how believers are to live. Hebrews 11 celebrates heroes of faith from the Old Testament and is prefaced with the powerful statement, "The just shall live by faith." The phrase, "The just shall live by faith," is mentioned four different times in the Bible. In Hebrews 11:6 it says that without faith it is impossible to please God. Faith is more than a moment. It is more than a movement. Faith is the lifestyle that pleases God.

A lifestyle is determined by the way a person lives. Many of us are familiar with New Year's resolutions. For many, a common resolution is to adopt a healthy lifestyle for the coming year. Although many start on the path toward a healthy lifestyle, they never actually achieve a healthy lifestyle (this pattern holds true for most such resolutions). A healthy lifestyle is not eating a salad one day, having portion control another day, drinking water one day, exercising another day, and every other day making unhealthy decisions. A healthy lifestyle is determined by what one does consistently. The power is in consistency.

It is the same with faith. Faith is supposed to be the lifestyle of the believer. One of the reasons I use *believer* as a synonymous term for Christian is to remind you that you are a believer. Believers believe. Since faith is supposed to be the lifestyle of the believer, it's impossible to please God without it, and it is vitally important in experiencing the superhuman life, we must take a closer look at faith.

Where Does Faith Come From?

We find our first piece in understanding faith in Romans 12:3, where the apostle Paul wrote:

> *For I say, through the grace given unto me, to every man that is among you, not to think of himself more highly than he ought to think; but to think soberly, according as God hath dealt to every man the measure of faith* (KJV).

In this passage, the apostle Paul was referring to Christians, so we can infer that God has dealt to every believer the measure of faith. Every believer starts out with the same faith. When people are born again, God deposits His faith into their hearts. Many Christians have said they wished they had the faith of a person they see as a superstar spiritual person. Only one thing separates them from the people they consider to have great faith—one group of people developed their faith, and the other did not. Faith is like a raw material; it must be developed. Faith is like a muscle; it must be exercised. Faith is like a seed; it must be tended so that it can grow to its fullest potential. You must develop your faith. You will not progress in your journey into the superhuman life further than the point to which you have renewed your mind and developed your faith.

Faith can be measured and quantified. In the gospels, Jesus commented concerning those who had little faith. He also commended those who had great faith. In fact, in speaking to the centurion in Matthew 8:10, Jesus said that He had not found great faith, like the centurion's, in all of Israel. Since Jesus used the word *found*, it implies that He was looking for it. Jesus even asked whether, when He returns, He will find faith in the earth (see Luke 18:8). Jesus is still looking for people with faith.

It would be an unfair of Jesus to judge concerning measurements of faith if people received different amounts of faith to start with. The centurion was commended because he used the faith that he had. Those who had little faith were tenderly rebuked, because their faith only lasted for a short time. The difference of great faith and little faith is determined by what people do with their faith. If people never develop their faith, they will never progress from little faith. Even worse than never progressing in faith, the person may fall into another category Jesus described—having no faith at all (see Mark 4:40).

As a believer, you already have faith. You must develop it and increase it. Romans 10:17 says, "So then faith comes by hearing, and hearing by the word of God." Faith must be developed and should be increased. If you want your faith to grow, you must put yourself in a place where you can hear the word continually. "Hearing and hearing" produces faith, not "having heard." Many have had faith concerning what God has accomplished in them through the marvelous work of Christ. They had faith in that work of faith, but they do not currently have faith in that work of Christ. How is that possible?

Spiritual growth is not always linear. When we think about growing and maturing, we think by a certain age a person should be able to do certain things. However, spiritually, that is not the case. A person could be saved for fifty years and still be a spiritual infant, while another person saved for ten years can be a mature elder in the faith. Hebrews 2:1 says, "Therefore we must give the more earnest heed to the things we have heard, lest at any time we should let them slip" (KJV). *Slip* means "to run out of a leaky vessel." Faith can come to us as well as leave us like milk runs from a slightly punctured jug. *Slip* also paints the picture of something drifting away.

Spiritual growth is not always linear.

Most of us, as children, spent time playing in a pool or ocean. If you did, you will remember how the toys you were playing with, if left alone, could drift away. The truth concerning new creation realities can drift away and slip our minds if we do not continually give attention to it. As the truth slips away, faith begins to leak. This should remind us how important it is to keep these truths at the forefront of our thinking if we want to live the superhuman life. If you rely only on what you have heard, your faith will leak, and these truths will slip your mind. However, if you continually hear these truths about what Christ has done in you, faith will continually come to your heart.

Notice that the Scripture said that faith comes by "hearing and hearing," not reading and reading. Faith comes to your heart as you hear. One of the reasons I encourage my congregation to read one chapter aloud a day is because faith comes by hearing repeatedly. Look at what God told Joshua before he lead the conquest of Canaan:

> *This Book of the Law shall not depart from your mouth, but you shall meditate in it day and night, that you may observe to do all that is written in it. For then you will make your way prosperous, and then you will have good success* (Joshua 1:8).

God's instructions to Joshua were clear. He was not supposed to let the book of the law depart from his mouth. In other words, he was supposed to keep saying it. The reason is simple—saying it aloud changed his mindset, showed him how to live, and built his faith. The book of the law was not just a list of commandments; this book also contained all the promises God gave concerning the promised land. The book of the law, Genesis to Deuteronomy, contained the stories of supernatural acts of God's power, provision, and deliverance. This book of the law was what Joshua needed to see, say, and hear on a regular basis in order to accomplish the superhuman feat of possessing the promised land.

The word *meditate* in verse 8 can also be translated as "to imagine, to meditate, to say, to study, to talk, to speak, to mutter, and to roar." Notice how many times it is translated in a way that means verbal communication. In context of Joshua 1:8, we see that God fully expected Joshua to study, to meditate, and to speak. In order to possess your promised land of the superhuman life, you must study, meditate, and speak concerning your new creation reality in Christ Jesus.

How then shall they call on Him in whom they have not believed? And how shall they believe in Him of whom they have not heard? And how shall they hear without a preacher? And how shall they preach unless they are sent? As it is written, "How beautiful are the feet of those who preach the gospel of peace, who bring glad tidings of good things!" But they have not all obeyed the gospel. For Isaiah says, "Lord, who has believed our report?" So then faith comes by hearing, and hearing by the word of God (Romans 10:14–17).

In the context of Romans 10, "hearing and hearing" also includes hearing the anointed word of God preached and taught. It is imperative that we continually place ourselves in a position to hear the word of God preached and taught. The preaching and teaching of the word encourages, strengthens, comforts, provides direction, brings faith, helps renew our minds, and so much more! Yet, how much a person receives from the anointed word that is preached or taught does not always have to do with the speaker, but the hearer. Throughout the gospels and Revelation, Jesus said, "He who has ears to hear, let him hear." Jesus was stressing the importance of the way that we hear.

"If anyone has ears to hear, let him hear." Then He said to them, "Take heed what you hear. With the same measure you use, it will be measured to you; and to you who hear, more will be given. For whoever has, to him more will be given; but whoever does not have, even what he has will be taken away from him" (Mark 4:23–25).

The measure, or the way, you hear the word will often determine how much you receive from the word. If you approach the hearing of the anointed word with an open heart, wanting to know more, you will receive more. However, look at the important warning of Jesus which reminds us that spiritual growth and understanding are not linear. In verse 25, Jesus said, "For whoever has, to him more will be given; but whoever does not have, even what he has will be taken away from him." Has what? What is the context here? The context is *whoever has ears to hear.* If you continually have ears to hear, you will receive more. If you stop having ears to hear, you are in danger of losing what you have already heard. Faith is determined by hearing and hearing, not just having heard.

"Hearing and hearing" also includes what the Spirit of God communicates to your heart. The Holy Spirit is the divine Helper; He has been sent to guide you, strengthen you, encourage you, comfort you, and empower you. In His guidance, He will speak to your heart in different ways. What He shares with your heart has the same ability to bring faith to your heart as the written word of God. The Holy Spirit will never lead you in a way that is contrary to the written word of God. He will always lead you in line with the written word of God. We must always put ourselves in the position to receive faith by hearing through reading the word aloud, by hearing the anointed word preached and taught, and by hearing the Holy Spirit speak the word to our hearts.

Lord, Increase Our Faith

And the apostles said to the Lord, "Increase our faith." So the Lord said, "If you have faith as a mustard seed, you can say to this mulberry tree, 'Be pulled up by the

roots and be planted in the sea,' and it would obey you"
(Luke 17:5–6).

Jesus had just shared with His disciples on how to handle offense and how often He expected His disciples to forgive others. What Jesus had shared was so overwhelming to them that the apostles replied, "Increase our faith," or as it says in the NLT, "Show us how to increase our faith." The response and parable that Jesus gave emphasize acting on what they had been taught. If you want your faith to increase, you must act on what you have already heard. Jesus' younger half-brother, James, shared on this important subject extensively in his epistle:

> *What does it profit, my brethren, if someone says he has faith but does not have works? Can faith save him? If a brother or sister is naked and destitute of daily food, and one of you says to them, "Depart in peace, be warmed and filled," but you do not give them the things which are needed for the body, what does it profit? Thus also faith by itself, if it does not have works, is dead. But someone will say, "You have faith, and I have works." Show me your faith without your works, and I will show you my faith by my works. You believe that there is one God. You do well. Even the demons believe—and tremble! But do you want to know, O foolish man, that faith without works is dead? Was not Abraham our father justified by works when he offered Isaac his son on the altar? Do you see*

that faith was working together with his works, and by works faith was made perfect? And the Scripture was fulfilled which says, "Abraham believed God, and it was accounted to him for righteousness." And he was called the friend of God. You see then that a man is justified by works, and not by faith only. Likewise, was not Rahab the harlot also justified by works when she received the messengers and sent them out another way? For as the body without the spirit is dead, so faith without works is dead also (James 2:14–26).

For faith to be effective and to increase, it cannot stay within the heart alone. The faith you have received may be acted upon. If you want to increase your faith, you must act on what you have already heard.

> For faith to be effective and to increase, it cannot stay within the heart alone.

The apostle James used two powerful stories from the lives of Abraham and Rahab. They had both heard from God. Abraham heard promises from God concerning his descendants. Rahab heard that God had given the land of Canaan to the children of Israel. The manifestations of those promises seemed unlikely for many different reasons. Yet, both Abraham and Rahab chose to believe God. They demonstrated their faith in God with corresponding actions. It was their faith married to their corresponding actions that produced the miraculous.

As James 2:17 says in the AMPC, "So also faith, if it does not have works (deeds and actions of obedience to back it up), by itself is destitute of power (inoperative, dead)." You must act on what you have heard from God. What action is required for faith to be operative? It depends on the situation, which is why I am so grateful we all have access to the divine Helper to lead us and guide us in every situation.

To help make your faith more operative concerning the new creation realities God has accomplished, I have written a few faith actions that you should implement every day.

It's Already Done: Saved, Righteous, and Redeemed

You are not an old sinner saved by grace. You are saved by grace. You are the righteousness of God in Christ Jesus, and you are the redeemed of the Lord. Since these things are already accomplished, faith is shown by your perspective, your lifestyle, and your conversation. The perspective of faith is to now consider yourself saved, righteous, and redeemed. No matter how you may feel, you are saved, righteous, and redeemed. You may wake up and not feel saved, but you know and believe the truth. You are saved, righteous, and redeemed. Whether the feeling is there or not, your action of faith is to act like you are saved, because you are.

Because you are righteous, when you sin, you do not run from God. You do not sink down in remorse and consider yourself a sinner. Since you are righteous, your action of faith is to boldly go to the throne of grace and confess your sin before Him and receive forgiveness and cleansing. Because you are redeemed from the curse, you refuse to accept the curse. When aspects of the curse appear in your life, you oppose it by declaring that you are redeemed from it and taking corresponding actions that align with your declaration.

For example, if you receive a negative report from the doctor concerning a certain sickness or disease, instead of thinking you will deal with this ailment for the rest of your life, you say, "I am redeemed from this." Your resistance to the disease is your thinking, your attitude, your words, and your actions. Because you believe you are redeemed from that disease, you begin to take steps to support a healthy lifestyle that enables your body to fight that disease. The words you speak are actions of faith. Eating healthy is an action of faith. Exercising is an action of faith. Taking proper care of your body is an action of faith. All of these actions are rooted in the truth of God's word: You are the redeemed.

You Are Forgiven

You are forgiven; God is not keeping a record of your sins. All of your sins have been washed away by the blood of Jesus. To what extent do you believe that you have been forgiven? Your belief in God's forgiveness has a direct correlation to your actions. Your belief in God's forgiveness goes farther than how quickly you go to Him after you sin. It goes farther than no longer considering yourself a sinner. How much you believe you are forgiven affects how you treat others, which is showcased in a famous parable of Jesus.

Then Peter came to Him and said, "Lord, how often shall my brother sin against me, and I forgive him? Up to seven times?"

Jesus said to him, "I do not say to you, up to seven times, but up to seventy times seven. Therefore the kingdom of heaven is like a certain king who wanted to settle accounts with his servants. And when he had begun to settle accounts, one was brought to him who owed him ten thousand talents. But as he was not able to pay, his master commanded that he be sold, with his wife and children and all that he had, and that payment be made. The servant therefore fell down before him, saying, 'Master, have patience with me, and I will pay you all.' Then the master of that servant was moved with compassion, released him, and forgave him the debt.

"But that servant went out and found one of his fellow servants who owed him a hundred denarii; and he laid hands on him and took him by the throat, saying, 'Pay me what you owe!' So his fellow servant fell down at his feet and begged him, saying, 'Have patience with

me, and I will pay you all.' And he would not, but went and threw him into prison till he should pay the debt. So when his fellow servants saw what had been done, they were very grieved, and came and told their master all that had been done.

"Then his master, after he had called him, said to him, 'You wicked servant! I forgave you all that debt because you begged me. Should you not also have had compassion on your fellow servant, just as I had pity on you?' And his master was angry, and delivered him to the torturers until he should pay all that was due to him. So My heavenly Father also will do to you if each of you, from his heart, does not forgive his brother his trespasses" (Matthew 18:21–35).

Often, when people read this parable, they remark, "How could this man not forgive this other servant, especially after all he had been forgiven?" Sermons often focus on the need to forgive others, since God has forgiven us of so much. Yet a question remains: Why didn't this man forgive his fellow servant? I believe the answer in found in these verses:

Then the master of that servant was moved with compassion, released him, and forgave him the debt. But that servant went out and found one of his fellow servants who owed him a hundred denarii; and he laid hands on him and took him by the throat, saying, "Pay me what you owe!" (Matthew 18:27–28).

After the servant was forgiven, what was the first thing he did? He found someone who owed him money. Notice what he did not do. He did not express gratitude or rejoice. What would you have done? Imagine if someone, moved with compassion, came to you and paid off all of your student loans, your car loan, your mortgage, and any other debt you may have.

Imagine another scenario. You have fallen on hard times. Bills are skyrocketing. Credit card debt is skyrocketing. Medical bills are piling up. You have not been able to make payments on your car, your student loans, or your house. You do not know what to do. You do not know where to turn. The situation is overwhelming. Then, out of nowhere, a generous philanthropist steps up and pays all of your debt. How would you react? You would be ecstatic. You would celebrate. You would be extremely grateful. The burdens and weight have been lifted off of your shoulders. You are free from the financial hardship that consumed your life.

If that would be your response, why did this man respond differently? The answer is in his response. The first thing he did was find someone who owed him money. The only reason you would do that is if you believed you still owed a massive amount of money. I do not believe the man in the parable was a bad man; he just did not believe he was truly forgiven. Since he did not believe he was forgiven, he tried to pay his debt off himself. Because he did not believe he was forgiven, he was harsh with his fellow servant, who had a financial hardship that was smaller than his. He did not extend mercy or grace, because he did not believe he was forgiven. Many believers treat people harshly because deep down they struggle with believing they are actually forgiven. Instead of being filled with love and compassion, they take a stand for truth and holiness in a way that comes off as harsh and unmerciful. If you truly let the revelation of God's forgiveness settle in your soul, you will be willing to extend that forgiveness to others.

Unforgiveness will shut down your faith, which is why Satan works tirelessly to keep believers offended. After teaching on faith in Mark 11, Jesus said, "And whenever you stand praying, if you have anything against anyone, forgive him, that your Father in heaven may also forgive you your trespasses" (Mark 11:25). Forgiveness is so crucial to your faith that Jesus said when you are praying, if you have anything against anyone, you must forgive them while you are praying.

Unforgiveness will keep you from experiencing God's best for your life. This is why, during our pre-message faith confession, I lead my congregation in saying, "I forgive everybody of everything." I encourage them to say it throughout the day, even if they are not dealing with offense or unforgiveness. I have them do this because it helps them practice forgiveness. The more you practice something, the more you are able to effectively execute it when the time comes. This faith confession also helps clear your heart and conscience from any unforgiveness that might be hidden in your heart.

A number of years ago, one of my deacons shared the following paraphrased story with me. He was going throughout his day and did what I teach concerning saying, "I forgive everybody of everything." Once he said that, he was reminded of a friend he had not spoken to in years. He began to remember that some type of offense had separated them. He called that individual, and God marvelously restored that relationship. This restoration flowed from the faith practice of operating in forgiveness.

You have the right to be mad at the person who offended you or did you wrong. However, staying mad, becoming offended, and operating in unforgiveness will rob you of the superhuman life. Believers are a forgiven people, and we must extend forgiveness to others.

Lord, Help My Unbelief

With all of these wonderful new creation realities and responsibilities, you may feel overwhelmed. A few of these may be hard for you to grasp and believe. What is the response of faith? We see that answer in a father who desperately needed a miracle during Jesus' ministry.

> *And when He came to the disciples, He saw a great multitude around them, and scribes disputing with them. Immediately, when they saw Him, all the people were greatly amazed, and running to Him, greeted Him. And He asked the scribes, "What are you discussing with them?" Then one of the crowd answered and*

said, "Teacher, I brought You my son, who has a mute spirit. And wherever it seizes him, it throws him down; he foams at the mouth, gnashes his teeth, and becomes rigid. So I spoke to Your disciples, that they should cast it out, but they could not." He answered him and said, "O faithless generation, how long shall I be with you? How long shall I bear with you? Bring him to Me." Then they brought him to Him. And when he saw Him, immediately the spirit convulsed him, and he fell on the ground and wallowed, foaming at the mouth. So He asked his father, "How long has this been happening to him?" And he said, "From childhood. And often he has thrown him both into the fire and into the water to destroy him. But if You can do anything, have compassion on us and help us." Jesus said to him, "If you can believe, all things are possible to him who believes." Immediately the father of the child cried out and said with tears, "Lord, I believe; help my unbelief!" (Mark 9:14–24).

The father of the young man was in a desperate situation. His son had been dealing with this affliction since childhood. The father was at the end of his rope and pleaded with Jesus saying, "*If You* can do anything, have compassion on us and help us." He hit the proverbial ball to Jesus, but Jesus immediately put the ball back in his court.

"*If you* can believe," Jesus replied, "all things are possible to him who believes." Throughout His ministry, Jesus credited faith for the positive outcome of prayer. In the gospels, we often hear Him say, "Your faith has made you whole." Faith allowed all of those individuals to receive their miracle. Jesus likewise challenged this father to use his faith. According to the words of Jesus, the deliverance of the child would not be possible if he did not believe. For the father to receive this miracle, he had to believe.

> When you see something concerning your new creation reality that is hard to believe, you need to respond in kind, saying, "Lord, I believe this. Help my unbelief."

"Lord, I believe!" the father cried, "Help my unbelief." The man released his faith when he called Jesus "Lord" and expressed his belief. As seen in Mark 9, the father received his miracle. The father showed the response of faith when it was hard to believe. He chose to believe anyway and asked for help in his unbelief. When you see something concerning your new creation reality that is hard to believe, you need to respond in kind, saying, "Lord, I believe this. Help my unbelief." When you pray that way, the Lord will respond, and He will help your unbelief. Unbelief, in this instance, is a lack of faith. How does Jesus help a lack of faith? We see one of those instances in Mark 6.

Then He went out from there and came to His own country, and His disciples followed Him. And when the Sabbath had come, He began to teach in the synagogue. And many hearing Him were astonished, saying, "Where did this Man get these things? And what wisdom is this which is given to Him, that such mighty works are performed by His hands! Is this not the carpenter, the Son of Mary, and brother of James, Joses, Judas, and Simon? And are not His sisters here with us?" So they were offended at Him. But Jesus said to them, "A prophet is not without honor except in his own country, among his own relatives, and in his own house." Now He could do no mighty work there, except that He laid His hands on a few sick people and healed them. And He marveled because of their unbelief. Then He went about the villages in a circuit, teaching (Mark 6:1–6).

Jesus returned to Nazareth and went to His home synagogue. Imagine the heart of the Lord. He wanted to do good in the area that He grew up in. Imagine how many times He had visited this synagogue while He was growing up. Now, He had been commissioned by His heavenly Father to go to this synagogue to teach and to heal. Imagine the excitement and compassion that was overflowing from His heart. However, the people at the synagogue that day did not receive what Jesus had for them. As Jesus began to teach, they began to question and become offended. In addition to their offense, they refused to believe.

The language of this verse is so powerful and jarring to religious notions concerning the ministry of Jesus. The Scripture does not say He would not do, it says, "He could do no mighty work there." He was only able to minister healing to a few sick people. Jesus was not able to do great miracles like He did in other cities because of their unbelief. Their unbelief was so strong that Jesus marveled at it. But Jesus did not give up. He responded to their unbelief by going around and teaching the word.

Today, Jesus will still help your unbelief. He will help your unbelief by taking you through the written word, communicating to your heart, and leading you to anointed preaching and teaching of the word.

Faith Is a Door

Faith is many things, including a door. It is a door that leads you into the superhuman life that allows you to experience new creation realities. If faith is not built up and increased to become a lifestyle, the superhuman experiences of believers will be limited to few and far between. About faith, Paul wrote, "For by grace you have been saved through faith, and that not of yourselves; it is the gift of God" (Ephesians 2:8).

When you were saved, you were born again and granted access to all of the new creation realities in Christ Jesus. You were granted access, but you still must go through the door. You were saved by grace through faith. Faith is the doorway to grace. Inside the marvelous grace of God is the superhuman life that has been promised to every believer.

Imagine it this way. Behind a simple garage door is your dream vehicle. A Mercedes S-Class. A Phantom Rolls-Royce. A rare Ferrari GTO. A Bugatti La Voiture Noire. An Aston Martin Lagonda Taraf. Take your pick; it's your dream car. All you have to do to get your dream car is go through the door; then it is yours to drive away. What is more valuable, the door or the dream car? The dream car, of course. The simple garage door is only worth a few hundred dollars. The dream car is worth six to seven figures. Although the vehicle is more valuable, you still have to go through the door to get it.

> The doorway of faith leads you to the superhuman life.

Here is the same question again, but in spiritual terms. What is more valuable, faith or grace? Grace, of course. Although grace is more valuable, you still have to go through the doorway of faith to get it. The doorway of faith leads you to the superhuman life. Continually increase your faith so that the door remains wide open, enabling you to continue your journey into the superhuman life.

Strong Faith or Weak Faith

How do you measure the strength of your faith? What is the sign of weak or strong faith? How much grace can your faith access? The life of Abraham, who is called the father of faith, gives us an accurate standard by which to measure our faith.

> *Therefore it is of faith that it might be according to grace, so that the promise might be sure to all the seed, not only to those who are of the law, but also those who are of the faith of Abraham, who is the father of us all (as it is written, "I have made you a father of many nations") in the presence of Him whom he believed— God, who gives life to the dead and calls those things which do not exist as though they did; who contrary to hope, in hope believed, so that he became the father of many nations, according to what was spoken, "So shall your descendants be." And not being weak in faith, he did not consider his own body, already dead (since he was about a hundred years old), and the deadness of Sarah's womb. He did not waver at the promise of God through unbelief, but was strengthened in faith, giving glory to God, and being fully persuaded that what He had promised He was also able to perform. And therefore "it was accounted to him for righteousness" (Romans 4:16–22).*

According to verse 19, weak faith is considering your circumstances. By this point in the scripture, Abraham was no longer a man of weak faith. He did not take into account the age or ability of their bodies. It was impossible for either of them to have a child. Yet, since Abraham was no longer weak in faith, he did not consider the impossibility.

In this verse, *consider* means to fix one's eyes or mind upon. Instead of considering his circumstances, Abraham considered the covenant God had made with him. He considered God's promise. He considered God's faithfulness. As verse 20 relates, he did not waver at God's promise to them. Instead, he gave glory to God. He praised God even when it did not look like anything was happening. Strong faith praises God in the face of contradictory circumstances.

There may be things in your life that seem to be a direct contradiction to the new creation realities God has promised you. Instead of fixing your eyes and mind on those things, be strong in faith. Choose to believe God, and say, "Father, I thank You that I am born again. Thank You for redeeming me. Thank You for making me a new creation in Christ Jesus. Thank You for Your anointing. Thank You for making me an overcomer and giving me the advantage. I choose to believe Your word!"

Faith Is a Substance

"Now the just shall live by faith; but if anyone draws back, My soul has no pleasure in him." But we are not of those who draw back to perdition, but of those

who believe to the saving of the soul. Now faith is the substance of things hoped for, the evidence of things not seen (Hebrews 10:38–11:1).

In the previous section on superhuman realities, we looked at the life that is possible to every believer. In a later section, we will examine more of the abilities and powers that accompany the superhuman life. These realities, powers, and abilities are things that people hope are real. Even if they do not think they are real, they enjoy watching these powers and abilities displayed on the small and big screen. The power and abilities that you have previously only hoped for are real; faith gives that reality substance in your life. Faith brings things that are only in the realm of dreams, wishes, and expectations into this reality.

Now faith is the assurance (the confirmation, the title deed) of the things we hope for, being the proof of things we do not see and the conviction of their reality [faith perceiving as real fact what is not revealed to the senses] (Hebrews 11:1 AMPC).

Faith is the title deed to the superhuman life. When people have a title deed, it shows that the object in question belongs to them. Faith is the confirmation that the believer can have a superhuman life. Sometimes, when you check into a hotel, the hostess will ask for your confirmation number. The confirmation number is the evidence that the hotel room has been reserved for you. Faith is the proof of the superhuman life. Faith's proof comes from continually hearing the word.

Challenges will at times present themselves as contradictions to the superhuman life God has promised you in Christ Jesus. Sometimes those circumstances will be so challenging that the only proof that you have a superhuman life is faith in the word. In those moments, you have to be like Abraham. Faith in what God has said has to be enough for you. You must consider your new covenant in Christ as greater than the contradictions you face. In those trying times, faith must be your evidence. Faith as your evidence will produce the supernatural in your life. As you continually study and meditate on what the word says about being a new creation in Christ Jesus, faith will rise in your heart and convict you that you have barely scratched the surface of the superhuman life. This freshly arisen faith will convince you that there is more for you and that you must embark on the journey into the superhuman life.

Faith Is Like a Vehicle

How far will your faith take you down the journey into the superhuman life? If your faith was like a vehicle, how fuel efficient would it be? It is important to build your faith, but you must also make sure your faith can take you into your future. Cars work by fuel. Whether you have a car that works by gas or electricity, the vehicle works by some type of fuel. The vehicle can only travel as long as the fuel lasts. If the fuel is efficient, the vehicle can go farther than it could if it was fueled by less efficient fuel.

In the same way, faith is fueled by love. Paul explained this when he said, "For in Jesus Christ neither circumcision availeth any thing, nor uncircumcision; but faith which worketh by love" (Galatians 5:6 KJV). Faith can only go as far as the operation of love in the life of the believer. Faith will only be as effective as the efficiency and quality of the love that is operating in the life of the believer.

In the comics, Superman's powers are derived from the rays of the sun. If Superman is ever in a weakened state or has had his powers drained, exposure to sunlight restores his powers. Just as Superman is recharged by the rays of the sun, a believer's faith is empowered by the revelation of the love of God and that love's operation in the believer's life.

SECRET 5

LOVE

And we have known and believed the love that God has for us. God is love, and he who abides in love abides in God, and God in him (1 JOHN 4:16).

D o you believe that God loves you? If you asked regular churchgoers that question, they may looked at you incredulously and say, "Of course He does." They may even quickly quote John 3:16, which says, "For God so loved the world that He gave His only begotten Son, that whoever believes in Him should not perish but have everlasting life." Others may even sing an old Sunday school favorite, "Jesus loves me, this I know, for the Bible tells me so."

God's love is supposed to be the bedrock of the Christian faith; it's elementary. However, many believers never let the reality of God's love for them settle deep into their hearts. They settle for mental assent of God's love instead of deep-seated belief in God's love for them. Mental assent of God's love will not take a person far in the journey into the superhuman life. It is a low-quality, inefficient fuel. A deep, accurate belief in God's love and its operation in the lives of believers will take them far in their journey into the superhuman life.

In 1 John 4:16, we find a pathway from mental assent to deep-seated belief. It says:

> *And we know (understand, recognize, are conscious of, by observation and by experience) and believe (adhere to and put faith in and rely on) the love God cherishes for us. God is love, and he who dwells and continues in love dwells and continues in God, and God dwells and continues in him* (AMPC).

Where is your belief in God's love for you? Is it mental assent or a deep-seated belief? This verse presents questions you must ask yourself; the answers to these questions will show you what you believe about God's love. How much of God's love do you understand? Can you recognize God's love? Are you conscious of God's love? What have you observed about God's love? What have you experienced of God's love? Have you put your faith in God's love for you? Do you rely on God's love for you?

Understanding God's Love

> *But God, who is rich in mercy, because of His great love with which He loved us, even when we were dead in trespasses, made us alive together with Christ (by grace you have been saved), and raised us up together,*

and made us sit together in the heavenly places in Christ Jesus, that in the ages to come He might show the exceeding riches of His grace in His kindness toward us in Christ Jesus (Ephesians 2:4–7).

The apostle Paul described God's love for us as *great,* which is defined as "large, abundant, and plenteous." The richness, or abundance, of God's mercy flows from His abundant and great love. This great love provided the grace that we have received by faith, and it has set us up for an eternity of experiencing the kindness of God. This great love made us alive with Christ, producing new creation realities within us. This passage makes it clear that mercy, grace, kindness, salvation, and newness of life in Christ Jesus are offered to us *because* God loves us. None of those things are based upon our works or because we deserve them. All of those things have been offered to us because of God's love.

To understand God's love, you must understand that God does not love you because you have done everything right. God loves you because you are you. You cannot increase or decrease God's love for you. He loves you! To believe that God's love for you is based on your actions or performance is to have a low quality and inefficient fuel powering your faith. This fuel will take you on the journey into the superhuman life, but your journey will be sluggish, because the faith vehicle will often break down and require more fuel. You must accept the truth that God's love for you has nothing to do with what you have done for Him. God's love for you is based on *who He is,* not on what you have done. When you begin to believe along these lines, your faith will be fueled in a more efficient way. God loved you so much that He granted you access to the superhuman life.

To believe that God's love for you is based on your actions or performance is to have a low quality and inefficient fuel powering your faith. This fuel will take you on the journey into the superhuman life, but your journey will be sluggish, because the faith vehicle will often break down and require more fuel.

Recognizing God's Love

In this the love of God was manifested toward us, that God has sent His only begotten Son into the world, that we might live through Him. In this is love, not that we loved God, but that He loved us and sent His Son to be the propitiation for our sins (1 John 4:9–10).

The love of God was shown to us in that God sent Jesus so that we might live through Him. The life that God provided for us in Jesus is the evidence of His love for us. Everything that has been made available for you as a new creation in Christ Jesus is because God loves you. The apostle John went even farther in identifying God's love by saying that God sent Jesus to be the propitiation for our sins. As our propitiation, Jesus became our atoning sacrifice. In other words, Jesus took our place. He suffered and died in our place. He paid the price for our sins so that we would never have to pay it. The superhuman life in Christ Jesus is a life in which believers will never have to pay for their sins. God did not do all of this because we deserved it, but because He greatly loves us.

Conscious of God's Love

How conscious are you of God's love in your everyday life? As we have seen in 1 John 4:16, believers need to understand, recognize, and be conscious of God's love by observation and experience. It is not enough to know about God's love; every believer needs to experience God's love on a daily basis. Experiential awareness is tied to acknowledgement. As it says in Proverbs, "Trust in the Lord with all your heart, and lean not on your own understanding. In all your ways acknowledge Him, and He shall direct your paths" (Proverbs 3:5–6).

To have experiential awareness of the love of God, you must recognize or acknowledge it on a regular basis. Acknowledging God's love is as simple as saying, "God loves me," or, "Thank You, God, for loving me." Other simple ways of acknowledging God's love include going over scriptures about God's love and singing scriptural songs about God's love. It is simple, yet profound. The more you acknowledge the love of God, the more you will grow aware of it and experience it. Every time you acknowledge

God's love, you are setting spiritual laws into motion and setting your mind on how much God loves you.

> The more you acknowledge the love of God, the more you will grow aware of it and experience it.

Have you considered purchasing a car? You may have selected the type of car you wanted in your mind. While you were searching for the best deal for that car, you may have visited several websites and dealerships. Then, as you went about your daily activities, did it begin to seem like you saw that car everywhere you went. They did not mass produce that car overnight. Instead, because you had set your mind on that car, you began noticing it everywhere you went. How much more would we recognize and experience God's love if we set our minds on it and acknowledged it? Consistently recognizing and experiencing God's love leads us to become more conscious of it in our daily lives.

A Prayer to Know God's Love

I often encourage believers to pray certain Scriptural passages on a regular basis. One of those passages contains a prayer that the apostle Paul prayed for the church of Ephesus. In this prayer, Paul prayed for the church to be able to comprehend the vastness of God's love:

That Christ may dwell in your hearts through faith; that you, being rooted and grounded in love, may be able to comprehend with all saints what is the width and length and depth and height—to know the love of Christ which passes knowledge; that you may be filled with all the fullness of God (Ephesians 3:17–19).

This is a prayer you need to pray for yourself, your family, your church, your pastor, and all the believers you know. I have changed the pronouns below to help you pray this prayer over yourself. Praying this prayer will help you grow in understanding God's love.

Father, I pray that I would become rooted and grounded in Your love and that I would be able to comprehend with all the saints what is the width, length, depth, and height of Your love. I pray that I come to know the love of Christ that surpasses knowledge so that I may be filled with the fullness of God. In Jesus' name, amen.

How Much Do You Believe God Loves You?

How much do you believe God loves you? Pause. Think about your answer. No, stop reading and actually think about your answer. Ready? How much do you believe God loves you? Do you believe you fall on a scale somewhere between the faithful foreign missionary and the unrepentant backslider, somewhere between the elderly intercessor and the holiday church attender? If you judge yourself on that scale, you are basing God's love for you on your works. God's love for you is not based on your works or your faithfulness.

The truth is—God loves you as much as He loves Jesus. "No!" You might religiously shout in your mind. "It can't be. Jesus is perfect. I'm not! God can't love me as much as He loves Jesus!" Jesus' own words can settle this discussion for us:

> *I do not pray for these alone, but also for those who will believe in Me through their word; that they all may be one, as You, Father, are in Me, and I in You; that they also may be one in Us, that the world may believe that You sent Me. And the glory which You gave Me I have given them, that they may be one just as We are one: I in them, and You in me; that they may be made perfect in one, and that the world may know that You have sent Me, and have loved them as You have loved Me* (John 17:20–23).

Did you see what Jesus prayed? He was praying for all those who would believe in Him through the words of His disciples. That includes each one of us. In this prayer, in verse 23, Jesus said that the heavenly Father loves us as much as He loves Jesus. Let those words of the Savior go deep into your soul right now. Pause. Think about it. Now, move past your insecurities and self-doubt and say the truth of the Scripture, "God loves me as much as He loves Jesus."

Saying that powerful statement of truth throughout your day will build your faith, renew your mind, and flush fear out of your spiritual system. Fear is more than fright. It is more than being startled by the unexpected. Fear is even more than being afraid. Fear is an operating system.

Phones, all types of handheld electronic devices, laptops, and computers all have a version of an operating system. An operating system is a software (instructions that tell a computer what to do) that controls the operation of a computer and also directs the processing of the computer's programs. Fear does the same things in people lives, even in the lives of believers. Fear gives instructions on how people should live their lives. If allowed, fear will control how people operate and will affect how they relate to everything in life. In 1 John 4:18, it says, "There is no fear in love." The AMPC continues the rest of the verse, saying, "Full-grown (complete, perfect) love turns fear out of doors and expels every trace of terror!" The more people grow in the revelation of God's love for them through understanding, recognition, and acknowledgement, the freer they become.

Growing and maturing in the love of God dismantles the operating system of fear and allows the operating system of wisdom to take its place. According to Hebrews 2:15, Satan enslaves and rules the lives of individuals through fear. Fear will keep believers from stepping out to experience the superhuman life. Fear will cause believers to close the door of faith and refuse to accept new creation realities. Where fear is tolerated, faith is contaminated.

> Growing and maturing in the love of God dismantles the operating system of fear and allows the operating system of wisdom to take its place.

You must allow the revelation of God's love to settle deeply in your heart until it drives out all traces of fear. This precious understanding of God's love will fuel and purify your faith. When we read of the heroic triumphs of the Avengers or the Justice League, we see that at times they had to overcome fear to deal with the challenges of the day. If they allowed themselves to stay in fear, they would not be heroes. Even worse, the people they were supposed to assist would suffer harm and loss.

How much more is that true for believers in Christ Jesus? How is this world suffering because believers are held captive by fear just like those who are still of the world? The fullest extent of the Christian life will not be realized if fear is tolerated. Fear must be flushed out! The more you grow in experiential awareness and knowledge of God's love for you, the less fear will have any type of influence over your life. As I will share in the next section, when fear has been dismantled, you will be able to live by the operating system of the wisdom of God.

Down In My Heart

I have the love of Jesus, love of Jesus,

Down in my heart, (where?)

Down in my heart, (where?)

Down in my heart,

I have the love of Jesus, love of Jesus,

Down in my heart, (where?)

Down in my heart to stay.

And I'm so happy, so very happy

I have the love of Jesus in my heart. (Down in my heart)

And I'm so happy, so very happy

I have the love of Jesus in my heart.[1]

As I typed these words, I could still hear these lyrics being sung in my head. Although these lyrics are primarily used for children's ministry, they contain a powerful scriptural truth that believers should carry with them their entire lives. The amazing love of God is already in the heart of every believer. As Paul said, "Now hope does not disappoint, because the love of God has been poured out in our hearts by the Holy Spirit who was given to us" (Romans 5:5).

God has poured the same love He loves you with inside your heart. The moment you were born again, you received the love of God in your heart from the Holy Spirit who lives in you. This love, within your spirit, enables you to do the impossible: love others the same way that God loves them. When people receive God's love in their hearts, they are now equipped to become conduits of God's love.

It is this love that enables you to fulfill Jesus' command: "Love each other. Just as I have loved you, you should love each other" (John 13:34 NLT). As Jesus said in John 13, the world will know that we belong to Jesus by the way we love. As Paul said in Ephesians 5:2, we are to "live a life filled with love, following the example of Christ. He loved us and offered himself as a sacrifice for us, a pleasing aroma to God" (NLT). When believers deviate from the life of love and the love that has been poured inside of them, they expose themselves to the believer's kryptonite.

Kryptonite

In the comics, Superman has near godlike abilities. They used to paraphrase the description of his powers by saying he is: "Faster than a speeding bullet. More powerful than a locomotive. Able to leap tall buildings in a single bound." On top of those abilities, he has super hearing, can fly, can freeze objects with his breath, can shoot lasers from his eyes, and is nearly invulnerable. Yet, this mighty hero is robbed of his great powers when he is exposed to kryptonite. Kryptonite, a crystalline material from Superman's original planet, releases a certain radiation that weakens Superman. In his weakened state, his powers are limited, and he is vulnerable like other mere mortals.

> In the same way that the love of God empowers believers like the sun charges Superman, strife robs believers of their power like kryptonite drains Superman.

Believers, born-again new creations in Christ Jesus, also have a kryptonite. There is something that robs believers of their God-given superhuman abilities. It causes them to stop experiencing new creation realities. It exposes them and makes them susceptible to the worst of the enemy's attacks. It makes them as weak as if they were mere mortals again. The believer's kryptonite is strife. In the same way that the love of God empowers believers like the sun charges Superman, strife robs believers of their power like kryptonite drains Superman. The New Testament church in Corinth is the perfect example of believers being drained of their superhuman abilities and becoming vulnerable to the enemy's attacks.

The ancient Greek city of Corinth was a cultural powerhouse, a center of trade, and a major Roman colony. Even in the midst of the loose morality of Roman society, Corinth was known for its more licentious living. In modern terms, it would have been a city where "if it feels good, do it" would have been the cultural mentality. In addition to the vice and promiscuity of the city, it was full of the worship of the Emperor and Greek and Roman gods.

This was the city where the apostle Paul visited in Acts 18 and planted a church. Paul, who usually did not stay in cities for long periods of time, stayed and taught in Corinth for over eighteen months. Many people were saved as the result of the apostle's ministry in that city. These believers formed a powerful church that overflowed in the gifts of the Spirit to the point that Paul said they came "short in no gift" (1 Corinthians 1:7). This is an amazing and notable feat. Every gift of the Spirit of God was operating in the church at Corinth and through its believers. However, trouble had been brewing. We see this in Paul's first letter to that church:

> *I appeal to you, dear brothers and sisters, by the authority of our Lord Jesus Christ, to live in harmony with each other. Let there be no divisions in the church. Rather, be of one mind, united in thought and purpose. For some members of Chloe's household have told me about your quarrels, my dear brothers and sisters. Some of you are saying, "I am a follower of Paul." Others are saying, "I follow Apollos," or "I follow Peter," or "I follow only Christ." Has Christ been divided into factions? Was I, Paul, crucified for you? Were any of you baptized in the name of Paul? Of course not!* (1 Corinthians 1:10–13 NLT).

Strife had been brewing in the Corinthian church, stemming from a debate over who was the best pastor and preacher. The apostle Paul had planted the church. Some of the believers had fallen in love with his style of preaching, teaching, and ministry. After Paul continued his missionary journey, Apollos came to Corinth and served as the pastor. His style was very different than Paul's. Apollos was known for his powerful eloquence, and a number of believers in the Corinthian church fell in love with his style. Somewhere along the way, the apostle Peter had also spoken to the believers in Corinth, and some number of them fell in love with Peter's style. Another group also formed, saying they only followed Jesus. These four groups began to bicker and fight until a civil war engulfed the Corinthian church.

This church civil war opened the door to the enemy and his deceitful tactics. In 1 Corinthians 5:1–3, Paul wrote:

> *It is actually reported that there is sexual immorality among you, and such sexual immorality as is not even named among the Gentiles—that a man has his father's wife! And you are puffed up, and have not rather mourned, that he who has done this deed might be taken away from among you. For I indeed, as absent in body but present in spirit, have already judged (as though I were present) him who has so done this deed.*

The apostle was saying that some Corinthian believers were sinning worse than the sinners in Corinth. This was not a quietly kept secret that no one else in the church knew about. It was public knowledge! These Corinthian Christians had given into a deception and believed they had a reason to be proud because of their acceptance and tolerance of this immorality.

The enemy's inroad with immorality was not the only inroad he made into the Corinthian church. The Corinthian church had been exposed to the radiation of kryptonite. They were in a weakened state. The apostle Paul mentioned this in 1 Corinthians 11:

> *For as often as you eat this bread and drink this cup, you proclaim the Lord's death till He comes. Therefore whoever eats this bread or drinks this cup of the Lord in an unworthy manner will be guilty of the body and blood of the Lord. But let a man examine himself, and so let him eat of the bread and drink of the cup. For he who eats and drinks in an unworthy manner eats and drinks judgment to himself, not discerning the Lord's body. For this reason many are weak and sick among you, and many sleep. For if we would judge ourselves, we would not be judged* (1 Corinthians 11:26-31).

When a person reads the phrase, "not discerning the Lord's body," some automatically think of the communion elements. Although those elements are included, if that is all a person thinks about, they are not fully discerning the Lord's body. Paul more fully defined the body of Christ just a little later on in this same letter to the Corinthians:

> *But now indeed there are many members, yet one body. And the eye cannot say to the hand, "I have no*

need of you"; nor again the head to the feet, "I have no need of you." No, much rather, those members of the body which seem to be weaker are necessary. And those members of the body which we think to be less honorable, on these we bestow greater honor; and our unpresentable parts have greater modesty, but our presentable parts have no need. But God composed the body, having given greater honor to that part which lacks it, that there should be no schism in the body, but that the members should have the same care for one another. And if one member suffers, all the members suffer with it; or if one member is honored, all the members rejoice with it. Now you are the body of Christ, and members individually (1 Corinthians 12:20–27).

The Corinthian church was not fully discerning the body of Christ because of how they were treating the other believers in their church. The issue they disagreed on was not a theological matter or a subject of great importance. It was a matter of personal preference that got out of hand and started a church civil war. As Proverbs says, "Starting a quarrel is like breaching a dam; so drop the matter before a dispute breaks out" (Proverbs 17:14 NLT).

Instead of agreeing to disagree about a matter of personal preference, the believers allowed the strife to grow to the point that it opened the door to Satan. In addition to the increased immorality, as 1 Corinthians 11:30 explains, many were weak, sick, and had died prematurely. This church of power now had become compromised in immorality, and its members were weakened, sick, and dying prematurely. Strife is as detrimental to the Christian as kryptonite is to Superman.

To avoid the kryptonite of strife, believers must forgive everybody of everything. As Paul said in Ephesians 4:32, "And be kind to one another, tenderhearted, forgiving one another, even as God in Christ forgave you." When people choose to hold onto offense and unforgiveness, they are choosing to willfully participate in the pathway that will lead them into strife. The more people rehearse the offense, or hurtful act, in their minds, the more upset and grounded in unforgiveness they will become. Eventually they will act on the unforgiveness in their hearts. Holding onto unforgiveness and offense is not worth missing out on the superhuman life. Strife is not worth the limitations of being only mere mortals. Forgiveness must be part of the lifestyle of believers in order to live the superhuman life.

Forgiving by Faith

"I want to forgive that person, but I just don't feel it. I don't want to be fake." Have you ever felt like that? The good news is, forgiveness is not a feeling; it is a decision. You can forgive by faith. The Bible commands us to forgive, and faith is in our hearts right now to forgive. Are you thinking about someone in particular right now? If so, you need to forgive that person. It's simple to do and can be done by faith. I have included a prayer for you to use below.

Heavenly Father, thank You for forgiving me of all my sins. Thank You for pouring Your love into my heart. I forgive this person (say the name or names). I let it go. Lord, heal my heart and help me to move forward. In Jesus' name, amen.

If you get mad all over again in five minutes, when you think about what they did, just forgive again and remind yourself, "I let that go." You should repeat this process until what offended you no longer traps you in unforgiveness. Forgiveness is the path to freedom. Refusing to forgive somebody is like drinking poison and hoping the other person gets sick. Do not cancel your journey into the superhuman life because you refuse to let offense go. The life God has for you is worth forgiving everybody of everything.

The Greatest Commandment

But when the Pharisees heard that He had silenced the Sadducees, they gathered together. Then one of them, a lawyer, asked Him a question, testing Him, and saying, "Teacher, which is the great commandment in the law?" Jesus said to him, "You shall love the Lord your God with all your heart, with all your soul, and with all your mind.' This is the first and great commandment. And the second is like it, 'You shall love your neighbor as yourself.' On these two commandments hang all the Law and the Prophets" (Matthew 22:34–40).

Walking in love is so important that Jesus referred to it as the greatest commandment. Living a life of love begins with receiving God's love or, as the apostle John wrote, "We love Him because He first loved us" (1 John 4:19). We are able to love God because He first loved us. Our love for God is shown by our obedience to Him (see John 14:21), and as Jesus said (and John reiterated in 1 John 4:21), our love for God should be closely followed by our love for others.

All of the commands and blessings of the law and the prophets are attached to the great commandment of love. The apostle James called it the royal law of love (see James 2:8). The love God has poured into our hearts is not meant to only stay in our hearts, but it is meant to flow to others. We are to be conduits of the love of God. As the apostle John reminded us, "Beloved, let us love one another, for love is of God; and everyone who loves is born of God and knows God. He who does not love does not know God, for God is love" (1 John 4:7–8).

The love God has poured into our hearts is not meant to only stay in our hearts, but it is meant to flow to others.

God Is Love

God is love, and He has commanded us to walk in love. Our love shows that we belong to Jesus. The love of God has been deposited in our hearts, and we are to love just like God does. The apostle Paul relayed this charge to the church at Ephesus:

> *And be kind to one another, tenderhearted, forgiving one another, even as God in Christ forgave you. Therefore be imitators of God as dear children. And walk in love, as Christ also has loved us and given Himself for us, an offering and a sacrifice to God for a sweet-smelling aroma* (Ephesians 4:32–5:2).

We are to be imitators of God just like little children imitate their parents. God is love, and that identity is one we have been divinely commissioned to imitate. If we are to identify as love, we must have a strong definition that gives life to that identity. The love we are called to identify with is displayed in 1 Corinthians 13:4–8:

> *Love endures long and is patient and kind; love never is envious nor boils over with jealousy, is not boastful or vainglorious, does not display itself haughtily. It is not conceited (arrogant and inflated with pride); it is not rude (unmannerly) and does not act unbecomingly. Love (God's love in us) does not insist on its own rights or its own way, for it is not self-seeking; it is not touchy or fretful or resentful; it takes no account of the evil done to it [it pays no attention to a suffered wrong]. It does not rejoice at injustice and unrighteousness, but rejoices when right and truth prevail.*

Love bears up under anything and everything that comes, is ever ready to believe the best of every person, its hopes are fadeless under all circumstances, and it endures everything [without weakening]. Love never fails [never fades out or becomes obsolete or comes to an end] (AMPC).

Love is patient and kind. Love is not jealous or boastful or proud or rude. It does not demand its own way. It is not irritable, and it keeps no record of being wronged. It does not rejoice about injustice but rejoices whenever the truth wins out. Love never gives up, never loses faith, is always hopeful, and endures through every circumstance (NLT).

This love is our identity, and 1 Corinthians 13:4–8 shows how we are to practically live in order to display it. Where are you challenged in your love walk the most? Place this passage of Scripture in a place where you can easily access it, and remind yourself of how you are supposed to live. Below, I've included a declaration of love for you to speak over yourself. I encourage you to declare this over yourself for the next thirty days.

I am patient. I am kind. I am never envious. I never boil over with jealously. I am not boastful or excessively proud of myself or my achievements. I do not display myself as arrogantly superior or disdainful. I am not conceited. I am not arrogant and inflated with pride. I am not rude and unmannerly. I do not act inappropriately. I do not demand my own way. I am not irritable or touchy. I am not distressed or restless. I am not resentful. I do not keep score concerning the wrong done to me. I do not rejoice with injustice. I rejoice when truth and what is right prevails. I never give up. I never lose faith. I am always hopeful. I endure through every circumstance. I never fail, because God's love is working powerfully and miraculously in me.

Saturated and Overflowing

The love of God has been poured out into your heart. The love you have received is not the only amount that is available to you. You can receive the love of God to the point that you are saturated and overflowing with God's love. This was the case for the church in Thessaloniki:

We give thanks to God always for you all, making mention of you in our prayers, remembering without ceasing your work of faith, labor of love, and patience of hope in our Lord Jesus Christ in the sight of our God and Father (1 Thessalonians 1:2–3).

The apostle Paul wrote to the Thessalonian believers just a few short months after he planted the church. While he was in Athens, he sent Timothy to check on the new believers and bring back a report concerning their life and spiritual growth. Timothy's report encouraged Paul, and the apostle responded by writing 1 Thessalonians. He began the epistle by sharing that he prayed for them often and remembered their work of faith, labor of love, and patience of hope. As he progressed through the epistle, he mentioned their faith and love again:

> *But now that Timothy has come to us from you, and brought us good news of your faith and love, and that you always have good remembrance of us, greatly desiring to see us, as we also to see you* (1 Thessalonians 3:6).

The apostle called Timothy's report about their faith and love "good news." This is not a church that was struggling with faith or love. Paul was encouraged by what he heard concerning those two areas, yet he prayed for increase:

> *Now may our God and Father Himself, and our Lord Jesus Christ, direct our way to you. And may the Lord make you increase and abound in love to one another and to all, just as we do to you, so that He may establish your hearts blameless in holiness before our God and Father at the coming of our Lord Jesus Christ with all His saints* (1 Thessalonians 3:11–13).

The Thessalonian church was already operating in love, but Paul prayed that they would increase and overflow in that love toward each other and everyone. The love of God that you are operating in and experiencing is meant to increase. There is always more of God's love for you to experience and more of God's love to flow through you. Paul made that clear when he wrote:

> *But concerning brotherly love you have no need that I should write to you, for you yourselves are taught by God to love one another; and indeed you do so toward all the brethren who are in all Macedonia. But we urge you, brethren, that you increase more and more* (1 Thessalonians 4:9–10).

Later in the epistle, the apostle once again celebrated the Thessalonian believers. He commented that they were taught by God to love one another. The love that this church operated in spread to believers throughout Greece. Although they were operating in a high level of love, Paul prayed that they would increase and instructed them to increase in love.

A few months after writing 1 Thessalonians, the apostle Paul penned 2 Thessalonians. What was the result of his interactions with and prayers for the Thessalonian believers? Did they increase in love? In fact, they did more than that!

> *My brothers, nowadays I thank God for you not only in common fairness but as a moral obligation! Your faith has made such strides, and (without any individual exceptions) your love towards each other has reached such proportions that we actually boast about you in the churches, because you have shown such*

endurance and faith in all the trials and persecutions you have gone through (2 Thessalonians 1:3-4 Phillips).

Wow! What an amazing and uplifting report! When reading 1 Thessalonians and 2 Thessalonians, many believers may be encouraged and even challenged to have faith and love like this first-century church. However, they may think that it would take decades to achieve what this wonderful church accomplished. The Thessalonian church achieved this in less than a year. Paul was with them for a few weeks before he had to rush to Athens. A few months after he left, he wrote 1 Thessalonians. A few months after that, he wrote 2 Thessalonians. If the Thessalonian believers could greatly increase in faith and love in such a short period of time, any believer can do the same.

How fast do you want to grow in faith and love? A lifestyle of faith and love pleases God and furthers your experience of the superhuman life. It all starts with a quality decision. A quality decision is supported by many daily (even momentary) decisions to continue in a life of love and faith. These decisions are backed by focus, prayer, and the words of your mouth. As you continually operate in the love of God, the love within you will grow. Walking in love, as well as all the operations of the Kingdom, is like sowing a seed (see Mark 4:26–29). After a seed is sown, as long as it is nurtured and cared for, it will grow and eventually produce fruit. Operating in love is the same. Choose to walk in love and keep making the decision to daily walk in love. Continue to focus, pray, and speak words over your life concerning walking in love. As you do these things, your love will grow and produce.

> A lifestyle of faith and love pleases God and furthers your experience of the superhuman life.

Many years ago, I was meditating specifically on the love of God. I constantly listened to messages concerning God's love. I put into practice the lessons I have shared with you in this section. As I listened to the messages and went over scriptures concerning God's love, I began to speak over my life words that lined up with what I was learning. One of the things I began to confess over my life was that people would be able to sense the love of God just by being in my presence. I did not tell anyone that this was a goal of mine or even something I desired. I only spoke these words in my private prayer time.

One Sunday, as I was heading into the church building, I stopped to talk with some gentlemen I had previously served with in a certain department in the church. As we caught up, one of the men said that he didn't know why, but every time I was around, he could sense the love of God. The other men with him agreed. Those words overjoyed my heart. I was seeing what I was believing for come to pass before my eyes. I was becoming a conduit of the love of God. God wants you to have similar experiences. I have included, below, a variation of what I speak over my life concerning God's love. For the next thirty days, I encourage you to speak these words over your life to activate the love of God within you.

> *My heavenly Father, the almighty God, love Himself, loves me. He loves me as much as He loves Jesus. He has poured out His love into my heart by the Holy Spirit, the Spirit of love, whom He has given to me. That love saturates every cell of my being to the extent that people can sense the love of God just by being in my presence. Today, I choose to be a conduit of the great love of God. I will love others the same way Jesus loves me. I love my family the way Jesus loves me. I love my co-workers as Jesus loves me. I love the brethren as Jesus loves me. I love my fellow humans as Jesus loves me. The love of God is overflowing within me. This love fuels my faith, and my faith grows exceedingly. This love flushes out all fear, because fear has torment. I believe God loves me, and I will love others the same way He loves me.*

Increasing in experiential awareness of and operation in the love of God will cause your faith to be fueled and efficient. Living this prescribed lifestyle of loving and experiencing God's love will cause you to be empowered and delivered from the effects of the kryptonite of strife.

Growing in love this way causes you to be positioned to be able to be "moved with compassion" as Jesus was when He performed the miracles in the gospels. Overflowing in love and faith will cause you to progress a great distance in the journey into the superhuman life. If you want to get the most out of this journey and experience consistent superhuman results, you must adopt the mind of Christ.

> Living this prescribed lifestyle of loving and experiencing God's love will cause you to be empowered and delivered from the effects of the kryptonite of strife.

Note

1. George William Cooke, "I've Got the Joy, Joy, Joy" (1925).

THE MIND OF CHRIST

*But the natural man does not receive the
things of the Spirit of God, for they are
foolishness to him; nor can he know them,
because they are spiritually discerned. But
he who is spiritual judges all things, yet
he himself is rightly judged by no one. For
"who hath known the mind of the Lord
that he may instruct Him?" But we have
the mind of Christ* (1 CORINTHIANS 2:14–16).

S ome superheroes are celebrated and admired, not necessarily for their superhuman powers, but because of how
they think. Batman is an example of this. In the comics, he
is a man who does not possess the powers of Superman or
the Hulk. He does not have the speed of the Flash. He has
access to great resources, but he does not have the various
abilities of mutants or meta humans. Many have access to

great resources, but what separates them from Batman is the way he thinks. In numerous comics, he is referred to as earth's greatest detective. Throughout different story lines, his strategy and advance planning saves the day. Despite his lack of superhuman powers, Batman is regarded as one of the greatest superheroes of the DC Comics; his character is ranked as high as Superman and Wonder Woman. It is Batman's mentality, discipline, and dedication that sets him in a class above many other heroes. With his mentality, he is able to marshal all of his resources to advance his crusade of justice.

In this book so far, we have covered the importance of hunger, reverence, faith, love, and understanding new creation realities. All of these things will help believers embark on and progress in their journey into the superhuman life. However, to get the most of out of this journey, believers must adopt the mind and mentality of Christ. In the same way that Batman is able to marshal all of his resources together, believers can marshal all of their vast resources together if they learn to think like Christ.

The things of the Spirit of God give the ability to live the superhuman life. As the apostle Paul said in 1 Corinthians 2:14, "The natural man does not receive the things of the Spirit of God." This is because "they are foolishness to him." The apostle continued, saying the natural man cannot know these things "because they are spiritually discerned." Who or what is the natural man? Why can he not discern the things of the Spirit of God?

> All people who are dominated by
> their flesh, their flesh's desires, and an
> unrenewed mind operate as natural people.

The natural man is the person who is dominated by his fleshly instincts and is governed by the desires of his flesh. This person is ruled by his five senses and his emotions. A person who is born again can still be a natural man or woman. This category is not reserved for the unregenerate. All people who are dominated by their flesh, their flesh's desires, and an unrenewed mind operate as natural people. Such people cannot understand or grasp the things of the Spirit; they consider those things to be absurd, silly, and foolish. Natural people cannot learn or understand these things, because they approach life with a natural mind. A natural mind, an unrenewed mind, considers the things of the Spirit absurd. The things of the Spirit have to be spiritually discerned. The Amplified Classic Edition says it this way, "He is incapable of knowing them [of progressively recognizing, understanding, and becoming better acquainted with them] because they are spiritually discerned and estimated and appreciated."

As Paul continued his epistle to the Corinthians, he made a powerful statement, "We have the mind of Christ" (1 Corinthians 2:16). Let that sink in. If you are a believer, you have the mind of Christ. Pause and say this out loud, "I have the mind of Christ." You really do. If you are a believer, you actually have the mind of Christ. However, the fact that you have something does not mean you use it. You can have a vehicle and never drive it. You can have money in a bank account and never spend it. You can have food in your refrigerator and never eat it. You can have the mind of Christ and decide to operate by the natural mind. What a sad state of affairs! How many believers have traded in the natural mind for the mind of Christ? If believers do not continually renew their minds, they will operate by the natural mentality instead of the mind of Christ. If you want to progress further in the superhuman life, you must embrace and operate by the mind of Christ.

> If you are a believer, you actually have the mind of Christ. However, the fact that you have something does not mean you use it.

The Operating System of the Mind of Christ

The operating system of the mind of Christ is the wisdom of God. The wisdom of God enables us to marshal the vast resources of new creation realities and deploy them accurately. Throughout the gospels, Jesus operated by the wisdom of God. Luke 2 describes Jesus' maturation into

His adult years as being "filled with wisdom" and "increasing in wisdom." When Jesus preached in His hometown, His critics asked themselves, "Where did He get this wisdom?" (Mark 6:2). Isaiah 11:2 prophesied that the spirit of wisdom would rest upon Jesus. In replying to critics of His ministry and methods, Jesus said wisdom is justified of her children or by the results it produces (see Matthew 11:19). Jesus operated on earth by the wisdom of God and gave us access to the same wisdom. The wisdom literature of the Old Testament gives insight into the wisdom believers have been granted access to.

> The operating system of the mind of Christ is the wisdom of God.

In Proverbs 1:7, it says, "The fear of the Lord is the beginning of knowledge, but fools despise wisdom and instruction." As I shared previously, the fear of the Lord is reverential awe and respect toward God, His word, and His ways. Reverence toward God precedes godly wisdom. This attitude and outlook toward God is the beginning of knowledge or information.

We live in an information age. Information runs rampant all around us. Our generation receives more information in a day then previous generations received in decades. Yet, in this information age, we have a rampant spread of information and misinformation. And some who have accurate information do not know how to apply it. What is the solution? Wisdom.

Wisdom is the correct application of knowledge. Wisdom is vitally important. As Proverbs 4:5–9 says:

> *Get wisdom! Get understanding! Do not forget, nor turn away from the words of my mouth. Do not forsake her, and she will preserve you; love her, and she will keep you. Wisdom is the principal thing; therefore get wisdom. And in all your getting, get understanding. Exalt her, and she will promote you; she will bring you honor, when you embrace her. She will place on your head an ornament of grace; a crown of glory she will deliver to you.*

Wisdom has the ability to preserve, guard, promote, and honor. As the principal thing, it is something believers must pursue. The wisdom of God allows you to decipher the map on the journey into the superhuman life. Proverbs 8 poetically shares more concerning the importance of wisdom and what it provides to anyone who would choose to live by it.

> *For wisdom is better than rubies, and all the things one may desire cannot be compared with her. "I, wisdom, dwell with prudence, and find out knowledge and discretion. The fear of the Lord is to hate evil; pride and arrogance and the evil way and the perverse mouth I hate. Counsel is mine, and sound wisdom;*

I am understanding, I have strength. By me kings reign, and rulers decree justice. By me princes rule, and nobles, all the judges of the earth. I love those who love me, and those who seek me diligently will find me. Riches and honor are with me, enduring riches and righteousness. My fruit is better than gold, yes, than fine gold, and my revenue than choice silver. I traverse the way of righteousness, in the midst of the paths of justice, that I may cause those who love me to inherit wealth, that I may fill their treasuries. The Lord possessed me at the beginning of His way, before His works of old. I have been established from everlasting, from the beginning, before there was ever an earth. When there were no depths I was brought forth, when there were no fountains abounding with water. Before the mountains were settled, before the hills, I was brought forth; while as yet He had not made the earth or the fields, or the primal dust of the world. When He prepared the heavens, I was there, when He drew a circle on the face of the deep, when He established the clouds above, when He strengthened the fountains of the deep, when He assigned to the sea its limit, so that the waters would not transgress His command, when He marked out the foundations of the earth, then I was beside Him as a master craftsman; and I was daily His delight, rejoicing always before Him, rejoicing in His inhabited world, and my delight was with the sons of men. Now therefore, listen to me, my children, for blessed are those who keep my ways. Hear instruction and be wise, and do not disdain it. Blessed is the man who listens to me, watching daily at my gates, waiting at the posts of my doors. For whoever finds me finds life, and obtains favor from the Lord; but he who sins against me wrongs his own soul; all those who hate me love death" (Proverbs 8:11–36).

Wisdom is the principal thing and produces elements of the superhuman life. As you read in Proverbs 8, it produces financial abundance that lasts. This wisdom produces a lifestyle of honor and righteousness. The wisdom of God is displayed in how He created the universe. Operating by the wisdom of God gives you the ability to correctly relate to the created world and live on a higher plane of existence.

Ecclesiastes 7:12 says that wisdom is a defense and that it gives life. The phrase "gives life" means that wisdom sustains life, preserves life, shields life, and saves life. Ecclesiastes 7:19 says that wisdom strengthens the wise more than ten strong leaders within a city. Wisdom gives believers the ability to have the superhuman lifestyle instead of only superhuman moments. Wisdom reveals what ability or resource is needed at the moment on your journey into the superhuman life. Without wisdom, it would be a guessing game of which resource and ability is required for superhuman success. Many people have inconsistent displays of power because of a lack of wisdom on what is needed in the moment.

Acquiring Wisdom

As I shared earlier, receiving knowledge, understanding, and wisdom begins with having reverential awe and respect toward God, His word, and His ways. Without this attitude and outlook, you will disregard the wisdom that God gives. In addition to having reverence, you must also request this wisdom from God. The apostle James gave clear direction on how to receive wisdom from God:

> *If any of you lacks wisdom, let him ask of God, who gives to all liberally and without reproach, and it will be given to him. But let him ask in faith, with no doubting, for he who doubts is like a wave of the sea driven and tossed by the wind. For let not that man suppose that he will receive anything from the Lord; he is a double-minded man, unstable in all his ways* (James 1:5–8).

James shared very simply that if anyone does not have wisdom, they should ask for wisdom from God. The apostle declared that God gives wisdom openly and abundantly. James 1:5 in the Phillips translation says:

> *And if, in the process, any of you does not know how to meet any particular problem he has only to ask God— who gives generously to all men without making them feel foolish or guilty—and he may be quite sure that the necessary wisdom will be given him.*

God will not rebuke you, reprimand you, or make you feel foolish or guilty in asking for wisdom. He loves to give wisdom, and He is glad that you ask for it. James continued his epistle by saying that when people ask for wisdom, they must ask in faith. What is asking or praying in faith? Jesus explained how a person should ask in faith in Mark 11:24, "Therefore I say to you, whatever things you ask when you pray, believe that you receive them, and you will have them."

Wisdom can be considered a thing in the context of Mark 11. When you ask in faith for wisdom, you must believe that you receive it. *Receive* means "to take, to catch, to claim, and to have." In other words, by the time you finish praying, you must believe you have the wisdom you asked for. Jesus said that if you pray that way, which is praying for things the word says you should pray for, you will have whatever you desire. How is faith displayed if you believe you receive what you asked for? What would you do if someone gave you a gift? The polite thing would be to say, "Thank you." In the same way, if you really believe you have received, you thank God for the wisdom He has given you.

The apostle James said that when people pray this way, they should "ask in faith, with no doubting." To doubt means to have an internal fight over what you are believing God for. What does an internal fight look like? After you have finished thanking God for the wisdom, you have a contradicting thought, *What if I don't figure out what to do? What will I do?* Instead of resisting that thought, you begin to dwell on it. Instead of saying in your heart, *God will show me what to do,* you begin to think, *I don't know what to do.* Eventually, those words come out of your mouth, "I don't know what to do. I can't figure it out. Why isn't this faith and wisdom stuff working?" That is doubting. You just finished praying a few moments ago and have already begun to doubt.

James compared people who doubt and waver to the waves of the sea. The waves go back and forth, back and forth, back and forth, as they are driven by the wind. Likewise, people who waver go back and forth, back and forth, back and forth, driven by their situation and their emotions. The apostle then followed up his comparison with a strong statement, "Let not that man suppose he will receive anything from the Lord."

Catch the Ball and Hold On to It

"Why won't they receive it? Doesn't God love them?" you may ask. Of course He does! It has nothing to do with God's love, but everything to do with their ability to receive. As I mentioned before, *receive* means "to catch." In a baseball game, if a ball is hit toward an outfielder, the outfielder must position himself to catch the ball. He will hold his glove and hands in a certain way to block out the sun and make sure the ball lands in his glove. After he catches it, he places his hand over the ball so he will not drop it. If the outfielder drops the ball, the person who hit the ball will not be out and will have a chance to score.

So many believers have caught the ball and then dropped it. Too many believers miss out on the superhuman life because they fumble the football of God's wisdom. They turn over the basketball of God's wisdom. You must catch the ball and hold on to it! Wavering will cause you to drop God's wisdom or anything else you ask God for. To avoid wavering, you must answer doubt with the word of God. You must fight words of doubt by speaking the promises of God. Thoughts of doubt do not cause believers to drop the ball; dwelling and acting on thoughts of doubt will cause believers to fumble every single time.

> Too many believers miss out on the superhuman life because they fumble the football of God's wisdom. They turn over the basketball of God's wisdom.

James continued his strong statement by adding, "He is a double-minded man, unstable in all his ways." In the context of this passage, a double-minded man is a person who goes back and forth from faith to doubt. People who waver from faith to doubt will be unstable in all that they do. Some believers have not found stability in the superhuman life because of their wavering. How can they find stability? The answer is simple: Become single-minded. If a double-minded man is unstable in all his ways, then a single-minded man is stable in all his ways. To be stable in all their ways, people must be singularly focused in faith. They must choose to believe God's word and resist the temptation to doubt and give in to the internal struggle. In these unstable times, the world needs stable, superhuman believers.

When praying for wisdom, be specific. It is good to begin your day praying for general wisdom for your day. After that, be specific in your request for wisdom. What do you have coming up that day that you will need wisdom for? Your relationships? Your kids? The meeting at work? An investment decision? A potential major purchase? Whatever it is, ask for wisdom for that specific situation; after you ask for the wisdom, thank God that He has given it to you.

The Spirit of Wisdom

As I shared previously, Isaiah prophesied that the Spirit of wisdom would rest upon Jesus. In his epistle to the Ephesians, the apostle Paul said that believers have access to that same operation of the Spirit of God and prayed they would receive it.

> *Therefore I also, after I heard of your faith in the Lord Jesus and you love for all the saints, do not cease to give thanks for you, making mention of you in my prayers: that the God of our Lord Jesus Christ, the Father of glory, may give to you the spirit of wisdom and revelation in the knowledge of Him, the eyes of your understanding being enlightened; that you may*

know what is the hope of His calling, what are the riches of the glory of His inheritance in the saints, and what is the exceeding greatness of His power toward us who believe, according to the working of His mighty power, which He worked in Christ when He raised Him from the dead and seated Him at His right hand in the heavenly places, far above all principality and power and might and dominion, and every name that is named, not only in this world but also in that which is to come. And He put all things under His feet, and gave Him to be head over all things to the church, which is His body, the fullness of Him who fills all in all (Ephesians 1:15–23).

In this prayer, Paul prayed that believers would receive many wonderful things. However, he began the prayer by praying that God would give them the spirit of wisdom and revelation in the knowledge of Him. This is a prayer that I pray frequently for myself, my family, my congregation, and many others. It is a prayer you should pray for yourself as well, so I have included it below.

Father, I pray that You, the God of our Lord Jesus Christ, the Father of glory, may give me the spirit of wisdom and revelation in the knowledge of You. I pray that the eyes of my understanding will be enlightened and flooded with light. I pray that I may know what is the hope and expectation of Your calling and invitation. I pray that I may know what is the abundance of the glory of Your inheritance within me and all the saints. I pray that I may know what is the exceeding greatness of Your power toward us who believe according to the working of Your mighty power, which You worked in Christ when You raised Him from the dead and seated Him at Your right hand, far above all things, and put all things under His feet.

I encourage you to pray this prayer daily, three times a day, for the next thirty days. Praying scriptural prayers has a profound impact on the life of the believer. Praying this prayer will grant you greater insight into God's ways and will grant you understanding in marshaling the vast resources available to you as a new creation in Christ Jesus.

Applying Wisdom

Jesus is the perfect example of using wisdom to apply the power of God accurately and effectively. As I shared previously, Jesus was moved with compassion and would produce the miraculous. Yet, Jesus did not automatically perform a miracle when He was moved with compassion. There was another step between the compassion and the miracle. This step was the wisdom and direction of God. Jesus explained this a handful of times in the gospel of John.

Then Jesus answered and said to them, "Most assuredly, I say to you, the Son can do nothing of Himself, but what He sees the Father do; for whatever He does, the Son also does in like manner. For the Father loves the Son, and shows Him all things that He Himself does; and He will show Him greater works than these, that you may marvel.... I can of Myself do nothing. As I hear, I judge; and My judgment is righteous, because I do not seek My own will but the will of the Father who sent Me" (John 5:19–20, 30).

For I have not spoken on My own authority; but the Father who sent Me gave Me a command, what I should say and what I should speak. And I know that His command is everlasting life. Therefore, whatever I speak, just as the Father has told Me, so I speak (John 12:49–50).

Do you not believe that I am in the Father, and the Father in Me? The words that I speak to you I do not speak on My own authority; but the Father who dwells in Me does the works (John 14:10).

A traditional, religious view of Jesus is that Jesus did whatever He wanted whenever He wanted because He was the Son of God. Yes, He was, is, and will always be the Son of God. However, Jesus did not operate on the earth as God. Jesus did not walk around and do whatever He wanted to do. To declare that He did is to make an unscriptural assertion that goes in the face of what Jesus said. In John 12 and 14, Jesus said He was not speaking His own words. He was saying what the heavenly Father told Him to say. In John 5, Jesus said He did what He saw His Father do. Jesus emphatically declared, twice, that He could do nothing by Himself. He added that He came to do the will of the one who sent Him.

Jesus would be moved by compassion, but He would not immediately act. Instead, He would see what His Father had to say about the situation or what His Father would show Him. How would He hear what to say? By asking His Father and listening for His response. How would He see what His Father would do? Within His heart with His spiritual eyes. The compassion of Jesus combined with the wisdom of God produced the miraculous. You can have the same results if you follow the same process and have the same mind. In fact, Jesus said, "He who believes in Me, the works that I do he will do also; and greater works than these he will do, because I go to My Father" (John 14:12).

To work the works of Jesus and the greater works, believers must adopt the mind of Christ and the operating system of the wisdom of God. In Philippians 2, the apostle Paul said,

> *Let this mind be in you which was also in Christ Jesus, who, being in the form of God, did not consider it robbery to be equal with God, but made Himself of no reputation, taking the form of a bondservant, and coming in the likeness of men. And being found in appearance as a man, He humbled Himself and became obedient to the point of death, even the death of the cross* (Philippians 2:5–8).

What mind, attitude, and perspective is the apostle speaking of? Jesus, although He was fully God, came to earth as a man. As a man, He humbled Himself and was completely obedient to the heavenly Father, even to the point of death. What is the mindset that we have to grasp? Humility and obedience. Humility, or being humble, is not thinking that you are a worthless worm. Humility is having an accurate opinion or view of yourself. Jesus had an accurate view of Himself, and He knew the mission the Father had sent Him to accomplish. Since Jesus had an accurate view of Himself, He was fully obedient to the heavenly Father.

Jesus did not operate on earth as God. He operated on earth as a man anointed by God. Although He was fully God, He operated as a man anointed by God. God does not need to be anointed, but humanity does. Jesus did not perform any miracles until after He was baptized and anointed with the Spirit of God in the Jordan (see Luke 3:22; Acts 10:38). After He was anointed, He began to fulfill His ministry and operate in the miraculous by saying what He heard His Father say and doing what He saw His Father do.

After I learned this in scripture, I made it my prayer before I would begin sharing a message. I pray, "Father, I need Your help. I only want to say what I hear You say. I only want to do what I see You do." I pray that way because I want the miraculous power of God to operate throughout the message and the entirety of the service.

See Things from His Perspective

If then you were raised with Christ, seek those things which are above, where Christ is, sitting at the right hand of God. Set your mind on things above, not on things on the earth (Colossians 3:1–2).

The mind of Christ and the wisdom of God will allow you to see things with the proper perspective. As new creations in Christ Jesus, we were raised with Christ. As the scripture says, we should seek, or set our attention on, heavenly things. Thinking in a higher way precedes higher results. If we set our minds on heavenly things, the things that are above, we will have heaven's results on earth.

As I have shared in different ways throughout this book, one of the biggest things that holds believers back from experiencing the superhuman life is their mindset. The Message version of Colossians 3:1–2 says:

So if you're serious about living this new resurrection life with Christ, act like it. Pursue the things over which Christ presides. Don't shuffle along, eyes to the ground, absorbed with the things right in front of you. Look up, and be alert to what is going on around Christ—that's where the action is. See things from his perspective.

> One of the biggest things that holds believers back from experiencing the superhuman life is their mindset.

If believers are to experience the superhuman lifestyle, they must learn to see things from Christ's perspective. They must see that all things are possible to the one who believes. They must see who they are in Christ Jesus. They must see that every problem they face is swallowed up in the great victory Jesus won for them in His resurrection. They must see things from Christ's victorious and enthroned position. As more and more believers adopt this mindset, the giants of our day will not even stand a chance!

The Right Wisdom

Who is wise and understanding among you? Let him show by good conduct that his works are done in the meekness of wisdom. But if you have bitter envy and self-seeking in your hearts, do not boast and lie against the truth. This wisdom does not descend from above, but is earthly, sensual, demonic. For where envy and self-seeking exist, confusion and every evil thing are there. But the wisdom that is from above is first pure, then peaceable, gentle, willing to yield, full of mercy and good fruits, without partiality and without hypocrisy. Now the fruit of righteousness is sown in peace by those who make peace (James 3:13–18).

As often is true, there is the real and there is the counterfeit. There are many different types of "wisdom" out there that believers may operate in. Just because people are saved, it does not mean they automatically operate by the wisdom of God. There are those who are hurt and bitter because of circumstances in life. They share their circumstances and warn that their situation will be everyone's result, no matter what they do. However, that person's operating system is not wisdom; it is their bitterness. Hebrews 12:15 says, "Look after each other so that none of you fails to receive the grace of God. Watch out that no poisonous root of bitterness grows up to trouble you, corrupting many" (NLT). Such people may be well meaning, but instead of healing from their hurt, they spread their bitterness and defile and corrupt many people. The apostle James described this type of wisdom in James 3. He called it "earthly, sensual, and demonic." This operating system produces bitterness and strife.

As James shared more concerning this counterfeit wisdom, he made a statement that mirrors what happened to the church of Corinth. When you read through 1 Corinthians, you can see the confusion that was present in the local church of Corinth. *Confusion* describes "a state of disorder, instability, and disturbance." As you continue through the epistle, you see the different evil works in the church that he had to correct. The kryptonite of strife will weaken believers, destabilize their lives, and bring confusion and all kinds of evil works.

In contrast to counterfeit wisdom, James said the wisdom of God is pure, peace-loving, considerate, reasonable, merciful, full of good fruits, unwavering, and always sincere. If your life is not producing the fruits described by the apostle in James in 3:17, you need to upgrade to a new operating system. The operating system of the wisdom of God will orchestrate a lifestyle of God's love and power in which you will be able to conquer every challenge on the superhuman journey.

Dwell

King David's strategy for living a holy lifestyle was to hide God's word in his heart. "Your word have I hidden in my heart, that I might not sin against you" (Psalm 119:11). By hiding God's word in his heart, the psalmist king was storing and treasuring the word within his spirit. As a pirate king would hoard up treasure and a big box store manager would well-stock his warehouse, David continually deposited the word of God within his heart. This is a strategy and example that every believer should follow.

Believers are not meant to live apart or detached from God's word. Believers are not designed to live with an intake of crumbs from the word of God. Believers are meant to be full to overflowing with God's holy word. The word is alive and full of power. It is the responsibility of all believers to make sure they are regularly receiving the word of God. All believers need to have a daily discipline of reading God's word. I encourage you to read one chapter aloud daily. All believers also need relationships with other believers who will encourage them in the word. Likewise, all believers need to be a part of a church where the anointed word of God is preached and taught.

We live in a time when technology has granted us access to so many different ways to receive God's word. We can receive it from a Bible app, a livestream, a podcast, and many other ways. All of those ways are wonderful and needed. Those wonderful ways are to be implemented alongside reading the word daily, having relationships with other believers, and faithfully attending church to hear the word preached and taught. If believers commit to following this strategy over a long period of time, they will have stored large amounts of the word in their hearts and will have furthered the process of renewing their minds.

The storing process, exemplified by David, leads believers to experience what the apostle Paul wrote in Colossians 3:16:

> *Let the word of Christ dwell in you richly in all wisdom, teaching and admonishing one another in psalms and hymns and spiritual songs, singing with grace in your hearts to the Lord.*

Paul's choice of the adjective *richly* describes the word dwelling in a person's heart in large quantities. This happens when people continually store the word in their hearts.

When they continually store the word in their hearts, it allows the word to dwell in them. The indwelling of the word influences the thinking, attitudes, and behaviors of the individual. This is why David chose this method as a path to right living; he understood that the word had the power to alter his behavior if he continually deposited that word in his heart. When the word is allowed to dwell in your heart, it will speak to you. Notice how the apostle said to let the word of Christ dwell in you richly *in all wisdom.* When the word is in your heart in large quantities, it will direct you and grant you wise insight into the affairs of life. The word you deposit in your heart will rise within you as you need it.

> The indwelling of the word influences the thinking, attitudes, and behaviors of the individual.

The psalmist king continued sharing about the importance and power of the word in Psalm 119. In verse 130, he said, "The entrance of Your words gives light; it gives understanding to the simple." The entrance, or the unfolding and opening, of God's word brings illumination. The more you place yourself in a position to read God's word, hear it preached or taught, and read teachings based on God's word, the more illumination you will receive. This illumination affects your insight into every area of life. Allowing

God's word to dwell in you richly will grant you illumination and understanding on how to properly apply the power of God to your situation to meet your need, overcome any circumstance, and defeat every giant. Wisdom needs to precede power in order for power to be used effectively. If wisdom is present, power can be applied effectively and be displayed to its maximum extent. Without wisdom, believers use all the power they have to power a lightbulb, when they could have used that same amount of power to illuminate an entire city.

> Adopting the mind of Christ with the operating system of the wisdom of God shows you how to administer the power effectively and allows the power to operate to its highest extent.

The journey into the superhuman life begins at the crossroads of hunger and reverence. Understanding new creation realities reveals who you really are and the map of the journey of the superhuman life. Faith grants you access to the power of the superhuman life, and love makes you efficient in the administration of that power. Adopting the mind of Christ with the operating system of the wisdom of God shows you how to administer the power effectively and allows the power to operate to its highest extent. Now that we have a working knowledge of all of those wonderful things, let's examine the explosive, dynamic, electrifying power that is available to every believer.

SECRET 7

POWER

It was the day of my graduation from Oral Roberts University. I had walked the staged, flipped my tassel, thrown and caught my cap, and was now celebrating and taking pictures with friends. One of those friends was originally from Paraguay, and we had traveled to Argentina together on a mission trip. His dad, a pastor of one of the largest churches in Paraguay, had traveled to neighboring Argentina and witnessed the power of God in operation in our lives.

As he congratulated us, he took me by the shoulders, looked square in my eyes, and said, "Kerrick, don't forget the power."

"I won't, sir," I replied. I did not, and I will not. The power of God at work has fascinated me as long as I can remember. As I shared in the introduction to this book, I remember as a child watching with great interest as I saw the power of God operating in my church. The fascination continued through my teen years. Every morning, before I went to school, I would watch Evangelist Benny Hinn's crusades and be encouraged by the miraculous healing power of God. I read and re-read books like *The Healing Anointing* by Kenneth E. Hagin and *The Anointing of His Spirit* by Smith Wigglesworth.

I would also watch and re-watch videos of men and women of God operating in the power of God. I remember one video by Reverend Tim Storey that I watched so often that I nearly had the entire video memorized, from his message to what he said as he prayed for people. As I grew older, I studied the lives of great men and women of God from the previous century—including Aimee Semple Mcpherson, John G. Lake, William Seymour, Maria Woodworth Etter, Jack Coe, and A.A. Allen, individuals who still inspire me to this day. Watching Kenneth E. Hagin and Oral Roberts minister left deep impressions in my heart and mind. I am grateful that I had the opportunity to meet both of those men of God.

All of those things and more from my childhood to my early adulthood caused me to hunger to see God's power operating in my own life. I loved what God had done in their lives, but I wanted Him to use me as well. While I was writing this book, I had lunch with a friend. We were discussing miracles of old and the lives of generals in the faith who had moved to heaven. In the conversation, he shared something he had heard at a conference that rung loudly in his heart. When he shared it with me, it rang as loudly in my heart. I pray it rings just as loudly in your heart. He said, "When will their stories become our own?" When will the stories of the explosive acts of the power of God become your own personal stories? This power empowers the new creation superhuman life and grants abilities that supersede the limitations of mere mortals. To better understand this power, I have categorized it into four areas: the power of privilege, miraculous power, the power of dominion, and the ability to produce results.

The Power of Privilege

But as many as received Him, to them He gave the right to become children of God, to those who believe in His name (John 1:12).

But to as many as did receive and welcome Him, He gave the authority (power, privilege, right) to become the children of God, that is, to those who believe in (adhere to, trust in, and rely on) His name (John 1:12 AMPC).

When you are born again and became a new creation in Christ Jesus, you are granted the privilege of becoming a child of God. This powerful privilege elevates the mortal life to a life of privilege and advantages. As I shared before, the new creation has the advantage in this life (see Gal. 6:15). In addition to the new creation realities we've already discussed, the child of God also has even more privileges and benefits. The apostle Paul shared about these privileges in Romans 8:

The Spirit Himself bears witness with our spirit that we are children of God, and if children, then heirs—heirs of God and joint heirs with Christ, if indeed we suffer with Him, that we may also be glorified together. For I consider that the sufferings of this present time are not worthy to be compared with the glory which shall be revealed in us. For the earnest expectation of the creation eagerly waits for the revealing of the sons of God (Romans 8:16–19).

The Holy Spirit gives evidence to all believers' spirits that they are the children of God. As children of God, they are also heirs of God. Many believers do not progress to the point where they receive the benefits of being heirs. They are grateful to be children, yet they do not live in or experience the fullness of being God's child. The apostle Paul said that not only are believers heirs of God, but they are also joint-heirs with Christ. Jesus did not make the Christian a lesser heir than Himself. He shares His glorious inheritance jointly with each believer. As heirs, believers have access to the ministry of angels.

Hebrews 1:14 declares that angels have been sent to serve, help, and minister to the heirs of salvation. Angels are beings of immense power, and all believers have at least one assigned to their lives. Many believers neglect the ministry of angels because they do not know that it is one of their privileges as heirs of God. Angels will assist believers as they walk out the plan of God for their lives and live out new creation realities. Part of one of the nightly prayers I lead my children in is, "Thank You for the angels that protect us."

We do not have to see angels to know that they are working on our behalf. Our primary job is not to see angels, but to follow the instructions of the Spirit of God. We are not promised to be able to see angels, but we are promised their ministry and assistance. Do not focus on trying to see an angel; instead, focus on being faithful to what God has shown you to do. Then you will be confident in angelic assistance in every arena of life.

In Romans 8, Paul spoke of the suffering of believers. This suffering is not sickness, disease, poverty, or depression. The suffering the apostle referred to comes from pressure-filled circumstances that confront believers because of their stand for Christ. These sufferings also include walking in love toward people during intense times of pressure. Included in the sufferings are the strong feelings often experienced while going through these intense times. These sufferings are the hardships and situations in life that believers undergo because of their faithfulness to Christ.

Notice, these are the sufferings that the believers go *through* or under*go*. These circumstances and situations are not permanent. They are temporary and subject to change. The end of the suffering is the faithfulness and delivering power of God. As promised in Psalm 34:19, "Many are the afflictions of the righteous, but the Lord delivers him out of them all." We will experience suffering in the Christian life; however, God provides victory for every pressured-filled situation. In the superhuman journey, you will run into giants and supervillains. However, because you are a new creation in Christ with all of the rights and privileges, you know that you will win. As Jesus said in John 16:33,

I have told you these things, so that in Me you may have [perfect] peace. In the world you have tribulation and distress and suffering, but be courageous [be confident, be undaunted, be filled with joy]; I have overcome the world. [My conquest is accomplished, My victory abiding] (AMP).

The victory that Jesus won for all believers is part of the inheritance of believers. As heirs, we are promised victory no matter what circumstances and situations we face. The victory is abiding, and we are more than conquerors.

In Romans 8, the apostle continued by saying that all of creation is waiting for the revealing of the sons of God. The whole earth is waiting for believers to live their privilege and no longer act as if they are mere mortals. The world has always longed for superheroes; it is time for believers to answer the call and be who they were born again to be. Paul continued this train of thought when, in Romans 8:29, he said that we are to be "conformed to the image of His Son, that He might be the firstborn among many brethren." Jesus came to earth as the firstborn, our example, our prototype. He left an example of love, humility, faith, wisdom, and power for us to follow.

> The world has always longed for superheroes; it is time for believers to answer the call and be who they were born again to be.

In Galatians 4:6–7, Paul continued to equate our status as children of God to heirs of God. He said,

> *And because you are sons, God has sent forth the Spirit of His Son into your hearts, crying out, "Abba, Father!" Therefore you are no longer a slave but a son, and if a son, then an heir of God through Christ.*

As children of God, the Spirit of God is continually reminding us of our Father and the relationship He desires to have with us. He reminds us that we are not slaves, but children of God and heirs through Christ. Previously, in Galatians 3:26–29, the apostle said:

> *For you are all sons of God through faith in Christ Jesus. For as many of you as were baptized into Christ have put on Christ. There is neither Jew nor Greek, there is neither slave nor free, there is neither male nor female; for you are all one in Christ Jesus. And if you are Christ's, then you are Abraham's seed, and heirs according to the promise.*

The privilege of being a child of God supersedes all of the class and caste limitations of people. In the end of Galatians 3, Paul said that being a child of God eliminates all of the class discrimination and limitation of race, nationality, gender, and economic status. Since believers belong to Christ, they are counted as descendants of Abraham and are also heirs to the promise of blessing granted to Abraham and his descendants.

Light Bearers

Therefore, my beloved, as you have always obeyed, not as in my presence only, but now much more in my absence, work out your own salvation with fear and trembling; for it is God who works in you both to will and to do for His good pleasure. Do all things without complaining and disputing, that you may become blameless and harmless, children of God without fault in the midst of a crooked and perverse generation, among whom you shine as lights in the world, holding fast the word of life, so that I may rejoice in the day of Christ that I have not run in vain or labored in vain (Philippians 2:12–16).

As children of God, we are granted privilege with responsibility. As Peter Parker's Uncle Ben said to him, "With great power, comes great responsibility." That saying guided Parker throughout his journey as Spider-man. The heart of the statement should ring true for all believers. We have been granted great privilege and power as children of God, and we must use it for the betterment of humankind and the world around us. Paul exhorted the Christians in the church at Philippi to work out their own salvation. The AMPC amplifies the understanding of Philippians 2:12 in this way:

> *Work out (cultivate, carry out to the goal, and fully complete) your own salvation with reverence and awe and trembling (self-distrust, with serious caution, tenderness of conscience, watchfulness against temptation, timidly shrinking from whatever might offend God and discredit the name of Christ).*

> We have been granted great privilege and power as children of God, and we must use it for the betterment of humankind and the world around us.

The salvation within you, everything that was deposited in you and changed in you when you were born again, must be cultivated and grown. The most spiritual point of your life should not be the day you are born again. That day is the start of your journey. Your journey should progress and reach greater depths and heights. If we consider salvation as a seed, we see that it must be cultivated in order to grow, flourish, and produce. All believers are responsible for the working out and cultivating of their own salvation. Our wonderful God has saved us, but we must use all of the wonderful, vast resources that He has placed within our spirits.

> The most spiritual point of your life should not be the day you are born again. That day is the start of your journey. Your journey should progress and reach greater depths and heights.

As we work out and cultivate our own salvation, Paul gave us an encouraging reminder—that God lives within us and is working within us to help us want to do what is right and to help us actually do what is right. The apostle continued his instructions so that the church of Philippi might show themselves:

> *Innocent and uncontaminated, children of God without blemish (faultless, unrebukable) in the midst of a crooked and wicked generation [spiritually perverted and perverse], among whom you are seen as bright lights (stars or beacons shining out clearly) in the [dark] world* (Philippians 2:15 AMPC).

The children of God are responsible to be light-bearers, those who shine and radiate the glory of God wherever they go. In Matthew 5, Jesus said that believers are the light of the world and are commanded to let their light shine in such a way that our actions will cause people to praise God. The Message translates Jesus' light-bearing instructions as:

> *Here's another way to put it: You're here to be light, bringing out the God-colors in the world. God is not a secret to be kept. We're going public with this, as public as a city on a hill. If I make you light-bearers, you don't think I'm going to hide you under a bucket, do you? I'm putting you on a light stand. Now that I've put you there on a hilltop, on a light stand—shine! Keep open house; be generous with your lives. By opening up to others, you'll prompt people to open up with God, this generous Father in heaven* (Matthew 5:14–16).

The lifestyle of love radiates the light of the glory of God. The apostle John encouraged believers to walk in the light as God is in the light (see 1 John 1:7). The more believers progress in the ways of God, the more their lives radiate His life. Proverbs 4:18 says, "The ways of right-living people glow with light; the longer they live, the brighter they shine" (MSG). God has provided so much for believers to walk in and experience in this life; many of us have barely scraped the potential of what it actually means to be new creations in Christ, children of God, and no longer mere mortals. The apostle John tapped into this line of thought in 1 John 3:

Behold what manner of love the Father has bestowed on us, that we should be called children of God! Therefore the world does not know us, because it did not know Him. Beloved, now we are children of God; and it has not yet been revealed what we shall be, but we know that when He is revealed, we shall be like Him, for we shall see Him as He is. And everyone who has this hope in Him purifies himself, just as He is pure (1 John 3:1–3).

It was the great love of God that conferred on us the honor of being children of God. We do not become children of God in heaven; every believer is a child of God now. It is so wonderfully marvelous that John pointed out how great God's love is to recreate us in this way. Yet, even though what we are now is marvelous, there is more for us in eternity. John said it has not been fully disclosed what we will be like when Jesus returns, but when He does return, we will be exactly like Him. This is what the Holy Spirit is consistently doing within us as He conforms us into the image of the Son.

The apostle Paul said in 2 Corinthians 3:17–18:

Now the Lord is the Spirit; and where the Spirit of the Lord is, there is liberty. But we all, with unveiled face, beholding as in a mirror the glory of the Lord, are being transformed into the same image from glory to glory, just as by the Spirit of the Lord.

The more believers look at Jesus through His word and their relationship with Him, the more the Spirit of God transforms them over a process of time. The process is described as being "from glory to glory." Believers can walk in various levels of experiencing the superhuman life. Believers work out their own salvation through various levels. Believers take what God put within them and cultivate it into maturity through various levels. Many believers do not progress past the elementary levels, when God has called them to be superhuman light-bearers who tackle the giants and issues of their day. The time must come to an end when believers make their homes on the ground level of salvation; the time has come for the revealing of the children of God who dare to trust God and live in the fullness of the power of the superhuman life.

> Believers can walk in various levels of experiencing the superhuman life.

Whenever believers take a stand for their rights and privileges as children of God, the enemy will challenge their stand to make them back down. If you have never exercised your rights and privileges as a child of God, the enemy seeks to apply pressure to make you believe that the beneficial rights and privileges do not apply to you. When the enemy challenges your rights and privileges, you must respond with the power of dominion.

> Whenever believers take a stand for their rights and privileges as children of God, the enemy will challenge their stand to make them back down.

The Power of Dominion

Humankind was created to operate in dominion. Humanity was created to dominate its surroundings, not be dominated. In the creation of humanity, God revealed that He intended for humankind to have dominion over the entire earth.

> *Then God said, "Let Us make man in Our image, according to Our likeness; let them have dominion over the fish of the sea, over the birds of the air, and over the cattle, over all the earth and over every creeping thing that creeps on the earth." So God created man in His own image; in the image of God He created him; male and female He created them. Then God blessed them, and God said to them, "Be fruitful and multiply; fill the earth and subdue it; have dominion over the fish of the sea, over the birds of the air, and over every living thing that moves on the earth"* (Genesis 1:26–28).

Psalm 8 refers to the creation of humankind. The psalm expands on God's original intent for humans to operate in dominion. It says:

> *When I consider Your heavens, the work of Your fingers, the moon and the stars, which You have set in place; what is man that You think of him, and a son of man that You are concerned about him? Yet You have made him a little lower than God, and You crown him with glory and majesty! You have him rule over the works of Your hands; You have put everything under his feet, all sheep and oxen, and also the animals of the field, the birds of the sky, and the fish of the sea, whatever passes through the paths of the seas* (Psalm 8:3–8 NASB).

God made humans to rule over all the work of His hands. He created it and then handed it over to Adam and Eve to rule and oversee. We know what happened—the Fall. Adam and Eve sinned; in their sinning, they transferred their authority to Satan, and he became the "god of this world" (see 2 Cor. 4:4). Instead of operating in dominion, humankind was now dominated by the devil. Satan, through the fear of death, enslaved all of humankind and kept them under his dominion (see Heb. 2:15). In the temptation of Jesus, Satan acknowledged the transfer of the power of dominion. Luke 4:5–6 says:

And the devil, taking Him up on a high moun-
tain, showed Him all the kingdoms of the world in
a moment of time. And the devil said to Him, "All
this authority I will give You, and their glory; for this
has been delivered to me, and I give it to whomever I
wish."

When Jesus came into the earth, He, as the second Adam (see 1 Cor. 15:47), operated in the dominion of the first Adam without the de-powering effects of Adam's sin. Supernaturally born of a virgin, Jesus was born free from the dominion of Satan and sin. In the midst of Satan's attempts to exercise dominion, Jesus exercised His higher authority. After Jesus resisted and overcame the temptation of Satan, Jesus returned to Galilee in the miraculous power of the Spirit. From that point on, Jesus demonstrated dominion over the forces of darkness and all of their works. One of the things that caused the people of Jesus' day to marvel at His ministry was the power of dominion that He operated in—His authority.

Then they went into Capernaum, and immediately on
the Sabbath He entered the synagogue and taught. And
they were astonished at His teaching, for He taught
them as one having authority, and not as the scribes.
Now there was a man in their synagogue with an
unclean spirit. And he cried out, saying, "Let us alone!
What have we to do with You, Jesus of Nazareth? Did
You come to destroy us? I know who You are—the Holy

*One of God." But Jesus rebuked him, saying, "Be quiet,
and come out of him." And when the unclean spirit
had convulsed him and cried out with a loud voice, he
came out of him. Then they were all amazed, so that
they questioned among themselves, saying, "What is
this? What new doctrine is this? For with authority
He commands even the unclean spirits, and they obey
Him." And immediately His fame spread throughout
all the region around Galilee* (Mark 1:21–28).

Jesus taught God's word with such authority that it
caused Him to stand out from the scribes of His day. Jesus'
authority-filled teaching provoked the unclean spirit within
a man who was attending synagogue that day. The demon
cried out while Jesus was teaching. The demon recognized
who Jesus was. Jesus silenced the spirit and told it to leave
the man. The spirit left the man in obedience to the word
that Jesus spoke. All who were in attendance were amazed
by what they heard and saw. The authority Jesus displayed
caused the whole region to be filled with reports of His
teaching and ministry. Immediately after this scene in the
synagogue, Jesus went next door to Peter's house. Luke 4,
Mark 1, and Matthew 8 each share what happened next:

*Now He arose from the synagogue and entered Simon's
house. But Simon's wife's mother was sick with a high
fever, and they made request of Him concerning her.
So He stood over her and rebuked the fever, and it*

left her. And immediately she arose and served them (Luke 4:38–39).

When evening had come, they brought to Him many who were demon-possessed. And He cast out the spirits with a word, and healed all who were sick, that it might be fulfilled which was spoken by Isaiah the prophet, saying: "He Himself took our infirmities and bore our sicknesses" (Matthew 8:16–17).

Then He healed many who were sick with various diseases, and cast out many demons; and He did not allow the demons to speak, because they knew Him (Mark 1:34).

The beginning of Jesus' ministry showcases the awe people had in response to His authority. Jesus used His authority and rebuked the high fever that was affecting Simon's mother-in-law. The fever bowed to Jesus' authority. That same evening, as the Sabbath had ended, people traveled to that house, bringing their sick and demonized loved ones. Mark said that Jesus did not allow the demons to speak, and Matthew added that Jesus cast the spirits out with His word. Throughout His earthly ministry, Jesus demonstrated dominion over demonic forces.

Delegated Authority

In Mark 6, the dominion Jesus operated in was expanded:

And He called the twelve to Himself, and began to send them out two by two, and gave them power over unclean spirits.... So they went out and preached that people should repent. And they cast out many demons, and anointed with oil many who were sick, and healed them (Mark 6:7, 12–13).

In Mark 6, Jesus delegated the power of dominion given to Him, as the anointed Son of Man and the second Adam, to His twelve apostles. As a result, they went out to different villages and had the same results that Jesus did in ministering to the sick and casting out demons. The delegated authority worked as if Jesus was actively doing the ministry Himself. "Well, that was because they were the twelve apostles," you might reason. Luke 10 shows another expansion of the dominion Jesus operated in:

After these things the Lord appointed seventy others also, and sent them two and two before His face into every city and place where He Himself was about to go.... Then the seventy returned with joy, saying, "Lord, even the demons are subject to us in Your name." And He said to them, "I saw Satan fall like lightning from heaven. Behold, I give you the authority to trample on serpents and scorpions, and over all the power of the enemy, and nothing shall by any means hurt you. Nevertheless do not rejoice in this, that the spirits are subject to you, but rather rejoice because your names are written in heaven" (Luke 10:1, 17–20).

The seventy were men and women of different professions and backgrounds. The common denominator was their belief in Jesus and their decision to follow after Him. When Jesus appointed these seventy individuals, He authorized them to operate in His power of dominion. He delegated authority to them in the same way that He had when He sent the apostles. As a result, the seventy returned with similar results. When they returned, they were celebrating and exclaimed to Jesus that the demons were subject to *them* through *His name.*

The demons had to submit themselves to the orders of the disciples because they were authorized representatives of the name of Jesus. The name is amazing, because of what it contains and who it belongs to. In expressing the greatness of the name, the apostle Paul said:

> *God also has highly exalted Him and given Him the name which is above every name, that at the name of Jesus every knee should bow, of those in heaven, and of those on earth, and of those under the earth, and that every tongue should confess that Jesus Christ is Lord, to the glory of God the Father* (Philippians 2:9–11).

The word for *name* includes the authority and character of that name. It is accurate to conclude that when the disciples said, "in the name of Jesus" they were also saying, "in the authority of Jesus." Everything they did after they were sent was as authorized representatives of the authority of Jesus. When they preached, they preached in the authority of Jesus. When they prayed for the sick, they did so in the authority of Jesus. When they cast out demons, they did so in the authority of Jesus. They were able to use the authority of Jesus because He had delegated it to them for their mission. Jesus did not delegate His authority and the right to use His name *only* to the twelve and the seventy. He also delegated His authority and the right to use His name to all who believe in Him:

> *And Jesus came and spoke to them, saying, "All authority has been given to Me in heaven and on earth. Go therefore and make disciples of all the nations, baptizing them in the name of the Father and of the Son and of the Holy Spirit, teaching them to observe all things that I have commanded you; and lo, I am with you always, even to the end of the age." Amen* (Matthew 28:18–20).

When Jesus said "Go therefore," He transferred the authority He had been given in heaven and on earth. The transfer of authority is also seen when He said to go, make disciples, and baptize in the *name* of the Father, Son, and Holy Spirit. In Mark 16:17–18, Jesus said:

> *And these signs will follow those who believe: In My name they will cast out demons; they will speak with new tongues; they will take up serpents; and if they drink anything deadly, it will by no means hurt them; they will lay hands on the sick, and they will recover.*

Jesus made it clear that these signs are not for a select few. These signs are meant to follow all who believe in Him.

In His name and authority, believers are able to operate in superhuman authority over sickness, demons, and deadly attacks, and they are granted the ability to speak with new tongues. This is delegated authority for the sake of the mission. You do not go out and pick up a venomous snake to display your authority. That is not operating in delegated authority; however, if you are ever in a situation like Paul was in Acts 28, you can shake the serpent off just like he did.

At different times in my life and ministry, I have used this delegated authority to minister freedom to others. As I relate a few of those stories, I want to point out that believers cannot be possessed with demons. The Holy Spirit indwells believers' spirits, and He does not allow roommates. I also want to point out that not every mental health challenge is a result of a demonic attack. I am grateful for anointed therapists just like I am grateful for anointed doctors. In the same way that not every physical sickness is the result of a demon, not every mental sickness or challenge is the result of a demon. However, Satan seeks to increasingly harass the minds of individuals. Beyond thoughts and ungodly mental strongholds, the enemy seeks to bind and torment believers in depression, oppression, and obsession. In cases like these, the enemy's evil spirits seek to hang on to or hang around the minds of believers.

On one such occasion, my wife and I were leading an experience at our church. We refer to our gatherings as experiences because we believe every time we gather, we are going to experience God by experiencing His word, His presence, and His love. In this particular experience, the Spirit of God directed us to call for those who were dealing with depression. Three ladies answered the call. While they were coming forward, the Spirit impressed on my heart that I was to tell spirits to "come out." I shared an abbreviated teaching with the congregation, explaining that not every mental health challenge is the result of a demon. Then, I walked down the stairs and gently laid hands on each of the ladies and simply said, "Come out." As I did, the power of God fell upon each of them, knocking them to the floor.

> The Holy Spirit indwells believers' spirits, and He does not allow roommates.

What causes this story to stand out in my mind is a letter I received not too many days after that experience. The letter was from one of the three women I ministered to. In the letter, she shared how she had been put on three medications to assist with her mental challenges. After the experience, she returned to the doctor who prescribed those medications. The doctor re-examined her and immediately removed her from two of those medications. She concluded her letter by sharing that she was believing to be removed from the third one in the very near future.

Over the years, the Spirit of God has directed me to minister in this way to those tormented by demonic nightmares and other things. In those times, I would order whatever spirit was tormenting them in the night to leave them alone, and as a result the individual would have sweet sleep. Another time in particular, I remember an individual who had not had quality sleep in days because of the torment of the enemy. At the altar, the Lord directed me, and I commanded all of the spirits that were harassing the individual to leave. This person was completely free, so free in fact that she experienced sweet sleep at the altar and eventually went home and had the best sleep she had had in a long while.

Another time, I was ministering in South Africa during a healing meeting. We were nearing the end of the meeting when a young lady came up on crutches. I had not called for her or for anyone else to come forward. As she approached the altar, I laid my hands on her and said, "Fix it, Jesus." Immediately, she fell to the floor and began to writhe under demonic oppression. I asked the pastor's wife to assist, and we immediately jumped into action using the delegated authority Jesus had transferred to us and declared peace over this young lady. After she was free, she walked perfectly without needing any assistance from the crutches.

As Paul said, we have been rescued from the authority of darkness and have been translated into the Kingdom of the Son of His love (see Col. 1:13). Satan and all of the kingdom of darkness cannot make believers do anything, because believers have been delivered from the dominion of darkness and granted their own dominion. The power of dominion that believers have received is far above all the powers and authority of darkness.

Seated

The apostle Paul shared insight into the authority of believers in Ephesians 1 and 2:

Which He worked in Christ when He raised Him from the dead and seated Him at His right hand in the heavenly places, far above all principality and power and might and dominion, and every name that is named, not only in this age but also in that which is to come. And He put all things under His feet, and gave Him to be head over all things to the church, which is His body, the fullness of Him who fills all in all. And you He made alive, who were dead in trespasses and sins, in which you once walked according to the course of this world, according to the prince of the power of the air, the spirit who now works in the sons of disobedience, among whom also we all once conducted ourselves in the lusts of our flesh, fulfilling the desires of the flesh and of the mind, and were by nature children of wrath, just as the others. But God, who is rich in mercy, because of His great love with which He loved us, even when we were dead in trespasses, made us alive together with Christ (by grace you have been saved), and raised us up together, and made us sit together in the heavenly places in Christ

Jesus, that in the ages to come He might show the exceeding riches of His grace in His kindness toward us in Christ Jesus (Ephesians 1:20–2:7).

The grandness of the dominion of power is represented by the seat of power. When Jesus ascended into heaven, He was seated at the right hand of the Father. The right hand is a place of privilege, power, and influence. His seated position showcases the height of His authority. As the apostle said, He is far above all principalities, powers, might, dominion, and every authority that is authorized in all ages. He put all of those powers and authorities under His feet. As the apostle Paul emphasized, Jesus is the head of the body of Christ. The feet are a part of the body. If those powers and authorities are under Jesus, and they are, then they are also under the Church, the body of Christ.

Paul echoed this sentiment when He stated that believers were made alive together with Christ, raised in Christ, and seated together in Christ Jesus. The delegated authority that believers have received flows from the right hand of the throne of the almighty God. This authority elevates believers to a level of superhuman authority that can defeat every challenge of the enemy. All believers are seated in Christ at the right hand of God and should get the same results as Jesus did when they use His authority. Satan does not always send possessed people to challenge the rights of believers; He sometimes sends demonic situations and circumstances to withstand believers. When those situations arise, we must resist those situations in the same way we would resist a demon-possessed individual.

Resist

James wrote, "Therefore submit to God. Resist the devil and he will flee from you" (James 4:7). Submission precedes resistance. If you are not submitted to God's word and will for your life, your resistance will be ineffective. What has the Spirit of God been leading you to do recently? If you focus on making sure you are yielded to what He daily directs you to do, you will find your resistance to the enemy infinitely more effective. When you resist the enemy, you are setting yourself against him and actively opposing him. Peter added, in 1 Peter 5:9, that we are to resist the enemy while standing firm and strong in our faith. What is the result of effective and firm resistance? Satan's forces flee. Satan and his forces will run in stark terror and try to escape believers who employ effective resistance.

It is possible to resist the enemy in one area of your life and let him run havoc in another area. To enjoy the full benefits of the superhuman life, you must set yourself against the enemy in every way he dares to show up and challenge you. I heard a statement from Pastor Nancy Dufresne that will help you understand the importance of resisting the enemy wherever he challenges. She said, "Anything you don't resist has permission to stay." What from the enemy are you granting permission to stay in your life? Rescind that permission by actively and firmly resisting the enemy.

Reign

For if by the one man's offense death reigned through the one, much more those who receive abundance of grace and of the gift of righteousness will reign in life through the One, Jesus Christ (Romans 5:17).

As I shared earlier in this book, you have been granted the status of royalty. Royalty reigns through decree. Remember, Jesus cast out the spirits with His word. He calmed the storm with His words. Permission is granted through action, inaction, and words. To reign in life, believers must follow the example of Jesus. When situations and circumstances arise to challenge your rights as a believer, look on the inside for what to say and what to do. As you speak the words you are given, you will get superhuman results.

Your words matter. They are important. Your words are carriers of power and authority. When a challenging situation arises, do not be loose with your lips. As the old saying going, "Loose lips sink ships." There is a hero in the Marvel Comics Universe called Black Bolt. His voice is so powerful that his mere whispers can cause widespread destruction. With such great power backing his voice, he is very selective about when and what he says. Just as Black Bolt is selective with the words he speaks, you must be selective with the words you speak. Your words matter and can affect the outcome of whatever you are facing.

Speak the words the Spirit gives you to say, and you will see His results. After you speak those words, do not back down from what you have spoken. You must stand firm in your resistance of the enemy and refuse to let the enemy convince you that you do not have any authority. When you speak the authorized words of the Spirit, they go to the root of the issue and then deal with the fruit.

In Mark 4, Jesus dealt with the source by rebuking the wind, and then He spoke calm to the sea. In Mark 11, Jesus spoke to the fig tree, and it dried up from the roots. Sometimes it takes time for words spoken to change the situation in such a way that you can see the change. Do not let time discourage you. Time is your ally, not your enemy. Stand firm during the time because you know you have delegated authority and are a child of God. The more believers position themselves to receive more of God's grace, the more they will see the effects of their superhuman royalty manifest throughout their lives.

The Power Is in the Consistency

I have heard this phrase throughout my life, and it rings true in a multitude of situations: The power is in the consistency. Believers need to consistently operate in the power of the dominion that has been delegated to them in order for it to have its maximum impact. One of the lessons Dr. Billye Brim has emphasized to me and others during recent times of ministry was the importance of daily taking our seat with Christ and ruling and reigning over the situations in our lives. Daily operating in your dominion is a way that you stand firm and resist the devil. It is not God's job to resist the devil in your life; it is your job. Below, I have included a way that you can daily exercise your authority.

> *Father, I take my place seated with You at Your right hand in Christ Jesus. I thank You for the privilege of this seat and the authority that comes with it. I plead the blood of Jesus over my life, spirit, soul, body, my family, my relationships, my finances, my property, everything I have, and everything that concerns me. I draw the blood line that the enemy cannot cross. Satan, I bind you. You cannot steal, kill, destroy, delay, or defraud me in any shape, form, or fashion. I bind you and curse all of your plots and plans to fail. No weapon formed against me shall prosper, and every tongue that rises against me I shall condemn in judgment.*

When I exercise my authority in this way, as I say *my family*, I pause and list my wife, my children, my family members, my congregation, and my ministry. There may be other things that the Spirit of God would prompt you to include in your list as you exercise your authority. Follow His leadings and promptings. As you progress in your superhuman journey, you will discover the vastness of this dominion. Glimpses of this dominion are displayed in the lives of men and women of faith throughout scripture. Whether it is shown as dominion over demonic powers, dominion over sickness and disease, Joshua's and Isaiah's dominion over time (see Josh. 10:12; Isa. 38:8), or Jesus' dominion over nature (see Mark 4:39–41; Matt. 14:25), the power of dominion that God has made available to His children is far above anything we have previously considered or imagined.

Miraculous Power

But you shall receive power when the Holy Spirit has come upon you; and you shall be witnesses to Me in Jerusalem, and in all Judea and Samaria, and to the end of the earth (Acts 1:8).

Before He ascended on high, Jesus promised that His disciples would receive power after the Holy Spirit came upon them. The word for *power* in Acts 1:8 means "miraculous ability, strength, might, and force." It is dynamic power. When Jesus referred to *virtue* (KJV) or power flowing out of Him, He used this word to describe that power. John the Baptist actively sought this experience of the Holy Spirit coming upon him and granting him miraculous ability, strength, might, and force.

"I indeed baptize you with water unto repentance, but He who is coming after me is mightier than I, whose sandals I am not worthy to carry. He will baptize you with the Holy Spirit and fire. His winnowing fan is in His hand, and He will thoroughly clean out His threshing floor, and gather His wheat into the barn; but He will burn up the chaff with unquenchable fire." Then Jesus came from Galilee to John at the Jordan to

be baptized by him. And John tried to prevent Him, saying, "I need to be baptized by You, and are You coming to me?" But Jesus answered and said to him, "Permit it to be so now, for thus it is fitting for us to fulfill all righteousness." Then he allowed Him. When He had been baptized, Jesus came up immediately from the water; and behold, the heavens were opened to Him, and He saw the Spirit of God descending like a dove and alighting upon Him. And suddenly a voice came from heaven, saying, "This is My beloved Son, in whom I am well pleased" (Matthew 3:11–17).

When John told Jesus that he needed to be baptized by Him, he was not referring to water. John was referring to the sermon that he had previously preached. John the Baptist wanted to be baptized by Jesus in the Holy Spirit and fire. He wanted the experience that Jesus later promised the disciples in Acts 1:8. As John testified in John 1:33, "He who sent me to baptize with water said to me, 'Upon whom you see the Spirit descending, and remaining on Him, this is He who baptizes with the Holy Spirit.'" John actively looked for this experience of being baptized in the Holy Spirit and fire. Fire is one of the ways the Holy Spirit's activity and power is described in the scripture. John the Baptist, according to Jesus, was the greatest prophet under the old covenant (see Luke 7:28). However, John knew that there was more, and now the more is available to all who are born again.

Within and Upon

Then, the same day at evening, being the first day of the week, when the doors were shut where the disciples were assembled, for fear of the Jews, Jesus came and stood in the midst, and said to them, "Peace be with you." When He had said this, He showed them His hands and His side. Then the disciples were glad when they saw the Lord. So Jesus said to them again, "Peace to you! As the Father has sent Me, I also send you." And when He had said this, He breathed on them, and said to them, "Receive the Holy Spirit" (John 20:19–22).

Although the disciples had received the Holy Spirit in John 20, Jesus still told them of a subsequent experience with the Spirit in Acts 1. When people are born again, the Holy Spirit moves into them, living on the inside of them. He is the agent of salvation and makes them a new creation in Christ Jesus. He lives within believers, enabling them to want to do what is right and helping them do what is right. He produces what is commonly referred to as the fruit of the Spirit in the lives of believers (see Gal. 5:22–23). Through partnership with Him, Christians work out their own salvation.

The opportunity to have the Holy Spirit living within us is new and distinct to the new covenant. In the Old Testament, the Holy Spirit only rested upon prophets, priests, kings, and those with a special assignment in a limited fashion. In the New Testament, people are given the gracious opportunity to have the Holy Spirit live within them and rest permanently on them. John the Baptist connected the baptism, or submersion, in the Holy Spirit with fire. Jesus, the baptizer in the Holy Spirit, equated the baptism with power.

Fire Power

One of the members of the Fantastic Four superhero team is called the Human Torch. Johnny Storm, the Human Torch, has the ability to transform his physical form into a fiery form. When he appears in the comics and movies, his appearance lives up to his superhero identity, a human torch. In a similar fashion, when believers are baptized in the Holy Spirit, they are covered in the Spirit to such an extent they resemble the Human Torch. When the 120 were baptized in the Spirit in Acts 2, individual flames rested upon each person.

Samson has often been thought of as one of the superheroes of the Bible. The Holy Spirit granted him superhuman strength and victory over all of his enemies. Samson's strength is usually the focus when people mention the power of the Spirit in his life. However, Samson had fire power as well. In Judges 15, after one of Samson's victories over the Philistines, the Philistines gathered their armies near the town of Lehi. The men of Judah were alarmed and asked the Philistines why they were setting up for war. The Philistines explained that they had come to capture

Samson. Three thousand men of Judah went and found Samson and told him that they had come to hand him over to the Philistines. Samson consented and made the men of Judah promise they would not kill him themselves. The men of Judah agreed and bound Samson with new ropes. As the men brought Samson to Lehi:

> *The Philistines came shouting against him. Then the Spirit of the Lord came mightily upon him; and the ropes that were on his arms became like flax that is burned with fire, and his bonds broke loose from his hands. He found a fresh jawbone of a donkey, reached out his hand and took it, and killed a thousand men with it* (Judges 15:14–15).

Samson breaking free and defeating one thousand men is a miraculous feat of strength. However, when we examine the scripture, we find another miracle also took place. The ropes that bound Samson suddenly became burnt fabric (flax), and his bonds broke loose. The phrase translated as *broke loose* actually means "melted." When the Holy Spirit came upon Samson, his chains melted and the rope was burnt so it was easy for him to break free. The fire of the Holy Spirit is powerful, and it granted Samson a great victory over his enemies.

The fire of the Spirit is also available to every believer through the baptism of the Spirit. When Johnny Storm wants to transform into his fiery state and use his powers, he says, "Flame on!" It is worth noting that, like David, Samson is listed in the Hebrews 11 Hall of Faith. Samson accomplished superhuman feats because he had faith in what God had said and how God had anointed him. His faith enabled him to be a superhuman. It is time for the body of Christ to do the same—to access the fire power of the Holy Spirit, follow Johnny Storm's example, and "Flame on!"

The Language of Another World

When the Day of Pentecost had fully come, they were all with one accord in one place. And suddenly there came a sound from heaven, as of a rushing mighty wind, and it filled the whole house where they were sitting. Then there appeared to them divided tongues, as of fire, and one sat upon each of them. And they were all filled with the Holy Spirit and began to speak with other tongues, as the Spirit gave them utterance (Acts 2:1–4).

The initial evidence of the baptism of the Holy Spirit and fire is speaking in other tongues as the Spirit supplies. (The Spirit supplies the manner or style in which the person speaks.) Every time someone received the baptism of the Spirit in the book of Acts, they spoke in other tongues. We see this with 120 disciples in Acts 2, with Cornelius and his household in Acts 10, among the disciples in Ephesus in Acts 19, and in the revival of Acts 8.

Looking more closely at Acts 8, we see that after Phillip preached in Samaria, many were saved, healed, and delivered, but the only one baptized in the Holy Spirit and fire was Phillip. Peter and John then came to Samaria for the express purpose of ministering the baptism of the Holy Spirit and fire to the new believers there.

Now when the apostles who were at Jerusalem heard that Samaria had received the word of God, they sent Peter and John to them, who, when they had come down, prayed for them that they might receive the Holy Spirit. For as yet He had fallen upon none of them. They had only been baptized in the name of the Lord Jesus. Then they laid hands on them, and they received the Holy Spirit. And when Simon saw that through the laying on of the apostles' hands the Holy Spirit was given, he offered them money, saying, "Give me this power also, that anyone on whom I lay hands may receive the Holy Spirit." But Peter said to him, "Your money perish with you, because you thought that the gift of God could be purchased with money! You have neither part nor portion in this matter, for your heart is not right in the sight of God. Repent therefore of this your wickedness, and pray God if perhaps the thought of your heart may be forgiven you. For I see that you are poisoned by bitterness and bound by iniquity." Then answered Simon and said, "Pray to the Lord for me, that none of the things which you have spoken may come upon me" (Acts 8:14–24).

When Peter and John laid their hands on the believers, they all received the Holy Spirit. Simon saw the initial evidence of the baptism, which led him to make a request with wrong heart motives. Before his conversion, Simon was the big shot in town because of the power of darkness he operated in. When Phillip came, he demonstrated power that was greater than anything Simon had experienced. Simon decided to follow Jesus, but he did not deal with the bitterness in his heart. Simon longed to be the big shot again, so he wanted to buy the ability from Peter. The motive of Simon's heart was the driving force of the rebuke from Peter. Simon was not trying to buy the gift because he desperately and hungrily wanted to be used by God; he wanted to be the big shot again. In the apostle Peter's rebuke of Simon, he told him that he did not have any part or portion in this matter. The word for *matter* relates to work, ministry, message, and utterance. The ministry, work, and message Peter and John came to share was the baptism of the Holy Spirit and fire. The utterance was the initial evidence of the baptism.

Another person recorded in Scripture as receiving the baptism was the apostle Paul. We know he spoke in other tongues because of what he wrote in 1 Corinthians. Speaking in other tongues was of great importance to the apostle Paul and many in the early days of the Church. It should be important to you as well. Speaking in other tongues is the initial evidence. It is just the beginning. Speaking in other tongues on a regular basis leads believers further down the journey into the superhuman life. It is the language from another world that grants otherworldly abilities and displays things that were previously hidden and secret. As Paul wrote:

However, we speak wisdom among those who are mature, yet not the wisdom of this age, nor of the rulers of this age, who are coming to nothing. But we speak the wisdom of God in a mystery, the hidden wisdom which God ordained before the ages for our glory, which none of the rulers of this age knew; for had they known, they would not have crucified the Lord of glory. But as it is written, "Eye has not seen, nor ear heard, nor have entered into the heart of man, the things which God has prepared for those who love Him." But God has revealed them to us through His Spirit. For the Spirit searches all things, yes, the deep things of God. For what man knows the things of a man except the spirit of man which is in him? Even so no one knows the things of God except the Spirit of God. Now we have received, not the spirit of the world, but the Spirit who is from God, that we might know the things that have been freely given to us by God. These things we also speak, not in words which man's wisdom teaches but which the Holy Spirit teaches, comparing spiritual things with spiritual (1 Corinthians 2:6–13).

The Holy Spirit reveals mysteries to believers. He unveils things that were previously hidden. God sent the Holy Spirit to us so that we can know the things that God has freely given to us. The Holy Spirit causes us to know who we are in Christ Jesus and everything He has made available to us as children of God and new creations in Christ Jesus. One of the ways He reveals things to us is through His words. When believers speak in other tongues, they are speaking out His words and mysteries:

> *For he who speaks in a tongue does not speak to men but to God, for no one understands him; however, in the spirit he speaks mysteries. But he who prophesies speaks edification and exhortation and comfort to men. He who speaks in a tongue edifies himself, but he who prophesies edifies the church* (1 Corinthians 14:2–4).

As believers speak in other tongues, they pray out divine mysteries, which are divine secrets, plans, and purposes. As they pray that way, they edify and improve themselves (AMPC), help themselves grow spiritually (TLB), and build themselves up (HCSB). The apostle Paul continued sharing about the importance of praying in other tongues and his personal practice throughout chapter 14.

> *For if I pray in a tongue, my spirit prays, but my understanding is unfruitful. What is the conclusion then? I will pray with the spirit, and I will also pray*

with the understanding. I will sing with the spirit, and I will also sing with the understanding. Otherwise, if you bless with the spirit, how shall he who occupies the place of the uninformed say "Amen" at your giving of thanks, since he does not understand what you say? For you indeed give thanks well, but the other is not edified. I thank my God I speak with tongues more than you all (1 Corinthians 14:14–18).

I thank God that I speak in [strange] tongues (languages) more than any of you or all of you put together (1 Corinthians 14:18 AMPC).

The apostle Paul said believers should pray in their natural language as well as in the Spirit (or in other tongues). He added that believers should also sing in their natural language and in the Spirit. The natural language is the language you use to converse every day. The language of the Spirit is the one He grants you as you speak in other tongues. In addition to praying out mysteries, there are times when speaking in other tongues is blessing, praising, or magnifying God.

Paul said that you can give thanks in a great way by only giving thanks in other tongues. However, it may not be the best way to give thanks if there others around who do not understand the place and importance of the language of the Spirit. The apostle then stated that he prayed in tongues more than any member of the church at Corinth and more than all of the church put together. Paul so greatly believed in speaking in other tongues that he outprayed an entire church that believed in speaking in tongues.

John G. Lake said that speaking in tongues had been the making of his ministry. His ministry was known for insight into the superhuman life given to believers and for outstanding miracles. Likewise, Oral Roberts would often credit speaking in other tongues with helping him learn how to build Oral Roberts University.

About speaking in tongues, or praying in the Spirit, Jude wrote:

> *But you, beloved, building yourselves up on your most holy faith, praying in the Holy Spirit, keep yourselves in the love of God, looking for the mercy of our Lord Jesus Christ unto eternal life* (Jude 1:20–21).

Speaking in other tongues builds up your faith. In the same way that you build up the power or charge the battery of your phone by plugging it into a power source, you also charge yourself and your faith by speaking in other tongues. Praying in the Spirit will elevate your journey into the superhuman life. The AMPC translates Jude 1:20, saying, "But you, beloved, build yourselves up [founded] on your most holy faith [make progress, rise like an edifice higher and higher], praying in the Holy Spirit." In Jude 1:21, it says that praying in the Spirit helps believers keep themselves in the love of God. Remember, God is love. The Holy Spirit, therefore, is the Spirit of love. When you pray in the Spirit, you are praying in the Spirit of love, which will help you walk in love toward others if you yield to the love.

Speaking in other tongues builds up believers and stirs them on the inside. It stirs up their hunger. It reminds them that the greater one, the Holy Spirit, lives within them. It stirs up their reverence. It also charges and builds their faith. Speaking in tongues helps believers stay in the love of God, connects believers to the wisdom of God, and produces power in believers' lives. The language of the Spirit is so wonderful! A lifestyle practice of speaking in other tongues will touch all seven secrets contained in this book.

Prayer Produces Power

My spiritual father, my uncle, Bishop Keith A. Butler, often says, "Prayer produces power. Little prayer, little power. Much prayer, much power. No prayer, no power." Prayer produces power. The apostle James shared this revelation in James 5:

> *Confess to one another therefore your faults (your slips, your false steps, your offenses, your sins) and pray [also] for one another, that you may be healed and restored [to a spiritual tone of mind and heart]. The earnest (heartfelt, continued) prayer of a righteous man makes tremendous power available [dynamic in its working]* (James 5:16 AMPC).

A lifestyle of continued prayer is a life that consistently accesses superhuman power. This tremendous, dynamic power enables the superhuman life to achieve feats that are beyond the scope of mere mortals. Having a lifestyle of prayer positions believers to hear clearly from God, pray out the mysteries and wisdom of God, strengthen themselves spiritually, and have a tremendous impact in the spiritual realm that ripples through the lives of those they are praying for.

Faith is the way believers access the power, but the power must be generated and made available. A phone has the capacity to be charged up, but if it never plugs into the power source, it will never operate the way it was intended. As believers progress in their superhuman journey and spiritual maturity, their spiritual capacity increases. As the capacity increases, it becomes necessary to charge more frequently, because power is now needed for many different areas. Spiritual maturity is marked by dependence. Progression in the superhuman journey should compel believers to pray more, not less.

Jesus, our perfect example and Savior, would often step away to pray and spend time with the heavenly Father. If this is the example He set for us, how could we ever think we would progress past the point of a life given to prayer? Prayer is more than a hashtag; it is communicating to and partnering with God. Believers who continually communicate with God and partner with Him in their praying will have access to tremendous, miraculous power.

Now to Him Who, by (in consequence of) the [action of His] power that is at work within us, is able to [carry

*out His purpose and] do superabundantly, far over
and above all that we [dare] ask or think [infinitely
beyond our highest prayers, desires, thoughts, hopes, or
dreams]* (Ephesians 3:20 AMPC).

The superabundantly, far over and above all that we ask,
think, pray for, want, think about, and imagine in the superhuman life is fueled by the power of God that is at work
within us. Notice that Ephesians 3:20 did not say according to God's power working in heaven or in other places. It
says it is according to God's power working in the individual. If people have little power working within them, they
will have a small portion of the over-and-above superhuman life. If people have more power working within them,
they will have a greater portion of the over-and-above
superhuman life.

Hunger, reverence, understanding and renewing your
mind to new creation realities, faith, love, and wisdom position believers to generate and operate in massive amounts
of power that will enable them to experience the superhuman life. As I have mentioned, these are not secrets that you
put into practice once. These are secrets that you put into
practice as a lifestyle, because the power is in consistency.

The Anointing

*How God anointed Jesus of Nazareth with the Holy
Spirit and with power, who went about doing good*

and healing all who were oppressed by the devil, for God was with Him (Acts 10:38).

Jesus was anointed when the Holy Spirit descended upon Him after His baptism. The anointing is the power of God, and it removes burdens, bondages, and yokes (see Isa. 10:27). As Peter said in his sermon in Acts 10, the news that Jesus was anointed spread around all of Judea (see Acts 10:37). One of the reasons this news spread so effectively was because this was one of the messages Jesus taught in the earlier days of His earthly ministry. It was the custom or habit of Jesus to share about the anointing the heavenly Father had placed upon Him.

> *So he came to Nazareth, where he had been brought up. And as His custom was, He went into the synagogue on the sabbath day, and stood up to read. And He was handed the book of the prophet Isaiah. And when He had opened the book, He found the place where it was written: "The Spirit of the Lord is upon Me, because He has anointed Me to preach the gospel to the poor; He has sent Me to heal the brokenhearted, to proclaim liberty to the captives and recovery of sight to the blind, to set at liberty those who are oppressed; to proclaim the acceptable year of the Lord." Then He closed the book, and he gave it back to the attendant and sat down. And the eyes of all who were in the synagogue were fixed on Him. And He began to say*

to them, "Today this scripture is fulfilled in your hear-
ing" (Luke 4:16–21).

Jesus quoted Isaiah's prophecy and explained that He was the fulfillment of that prophecy. Christ is not Jesus' last name; it is his epithet that describes a quality or characteristic. *Christ* means "the anointed." Jesus Christ is another way to say Jesus the Anointed One of God. When believers refer to themselves as Christians, they are identifying with Jesus and His anointing. They are acknowledging that they too have been anointed by God because of their relationship to Jesus. All believers have been anointed in a general way.

The Bible also tells us about specific anointing or graces given to believers to accomplish certain assignments from God. The anointing has different levels and measures. Jesus operated in the anointing of the Spirit without measure, because He spoke the words God gave Him (see John 3:34), loved righteousness, and was completely opposed to iniquity (see Heb. 1:9). As believers continue their superhuman journey and yield to God's will and ways, they will be granted greater anointing.

The psalmist wrote, "But my horn You have exalted like a wild ox; I have been anointed with fresh oil" (Psalm 92:10). Every day you walk with God, He has fresh anointing oil of His Spirit to place upon your life. You are not limited to the anointing you have experienced in the past. He always makes more anointing available to believers if they dare to use what they have been given and hunger for more.

The Glory Is in You

One of the amazing characteristics associated with many of God's appearances in the Old Testament is the manifestation of His glory and power. Moses and the children of Israel saw it as fire, smoke, a bright cloud, a thick storm cloud, and lightning, and they heard a loud noise and the sound of a trumpet (see Exod. 19). Solomon and the people of his day saw it as a thick storm cloud and fire as it filled the temple (see 2 Chron. 5; 7). Isaiah described it as light (see Isa. 60:1). This is the powerful glory of the heavenly Father.

The first miracle that Jesus performed, the turning of water into wine, is described in John as a manifestation of His glory: "This beginning of signs Jesus did in Cana of Galilee, and manifested His glory; and His disciples believed in Him" (John 2:11). The acts of power that Jesus did in His earthly ministry were manifestations of the glory. In His prayer in John 17:22, Jesus prayed, "And the glory which You gave Me I have given them, that they may be one just as We are one." The glory of the heavenly Father, which was seen in the Old Testament, manifested through Jesus as miracles, signs, wonders, and great deliverances. In this prayer, Jesus said He gave that same glory to believers. Even the fire of the baptism of the Holy Spirit and fire is a manifestation of the glory of God!

This is a new creation reality that we must come to grips with—we are carriers of the glory of God and should expect it to manifest in our lives. The apostle Paul called this amazing truth a mystery that he had been called to make known among the Gentiles. He said, "To whom God willed to make known what the wealth of the glory of this mystery among the Gentiles is, the mystery that is Christ in you, the hope of glory" (Colossians 1:27 NASB). The mystery revealed is this: Since Christ lives in you, He is your hope of glory. Hope is a positive expectation of good. Since Christ lives in you, you can increasingly expect to experience more of God's glory in your life.

Part of Paul's prayer in Ephesians 1:18 is that we "may know what is the hope of His calling, what are the riches of the glory of His inheritance in the saints." The abundance of the glory of God is within all believers. The vast resources of the new creation are within the spirits of all believers. Paul prayed in this passage that believers would come to intimately understand and have a working knowledge of what God has already placed on the inside of them when they were born again. As you pray the Ephesians 1 prayer, you will develop a working knowledge of what God has placed in you and how you can manifest that glory throughout your superhuman journey.

Contact and Transmission

As anointed carriers of God's glory and miraculous power, how do believers release what is within them and upon them? We have seen examples already of power demonstrated by speaking. This power is so real and tangible that at certain levels of operation it can flow from one person to another and from one person into certain objects. The book of Acts shares two of those experiences, one about Paul and one about Peter. Of Paul, we read:

Now God worked unusual miracles by the hands of Paul, so that even handkerchiefs or aprons were brought from his body to the sick, and the diseases left them and the evil spirits went out of them (Acts 19:11–12).

The apostle Paul worked many miracles throughout his ministry. However, Luke, the writer of Acts, noted that these were special and unusual miracles. This was a time when the power of God was operating at a higher level and measure than Paul had previously experienced. When handkerchiefs or aprons, everyday objects of cloth, came into contact with Paul, the miraculous power would flow from him into these objects. These objects then became storage batteries of the power of God. When the sick or possessed were touched by these storage batteries, they were all healed.

I have had times in my life and ministry so far when the power of God was operating at a high level. After one particular service in Texas, I had finished ministering to people, but I could still sense the presence of God in a strong way. I could feel it as if it were fire flowing from my hands. I was on my way to a restaurant for lunch with my fiancée (soon to be wife) and a close friend, and I tried to explain to them what I was experiencing. While we were in the car, I asked them to put their hands about one foot from my hands. They did, and they both said they could feel the power of God flowing from me into their hands. The next day, as I was deciding which clothes needed to go to the cleaners, I touched the shirt I had worn the previous day. Immediately, I felt the presence of God go into my hands. The power I had operated under the day before had radiated in a measure onto the shirt I was wearing.

At times since then, when I have known I was under a greater operation of the power of God, I have prayed over handkerchiefs, pieces of cloth, or other objects. I have heard back testimonies from miles and states away of the supernatural occurrences that happened when those objects arrived to those who needed them. Whenever the power of God is working on that level within you, it can be transmitted into objects through contact.

Peter's experience of this greater anointing was similar:

And through the hands of the apostles many signs and wonders were done among the people. And they were all with one accord in Solomon's Porch. Yet none of the rest dared join them, but the people esteemed them highly. And believers were increasingly added to the Lord, multitudes of both men and women, so that they brought the sick out into the streets and laid them on beds and couches, that at least the shadow of Peter passing by might fall on some of them. Also a multitude gathered from the surrounding cities to

Jerusalem, bringing sick people and those who were tormented by unclean spirits, and they were all healed (Acts 5:12–16).

Peter's shadow is not what is special in Acts 5, just like handkerchiefs and aprons were not special in Acts 19. What was special was the miraculous power that was flowing through and radiating from Peter. During this time, if people could get within the general radius of Peter's shadow, they would be healed. It was not the shadow that healed them. It was the power of God operating at such a high level that if people came close to Peter they would be healed. There is a flow of this miraculous power that can manifest itself in creative and wonderful ways. In Luke 6, we see times in Jesus' ministry when this miraculous power flowed out of Him. During this time, if anyone touched Him, the power would flow out of Him and bring healing and deliverance.

I remember a time when I had the opportunity to minister with a team in Buenos Aires, Argentina. During the two weeks of ministry, we would pray for people late into the night. On one of these nights, the power and the glory of God was operating at a higher level. Our team had broken up into different groups to pray for those who requested prayer. As people approached my friend and me for prayer, before they could get close, the power of God would encounter them, and they would fall upon the floor. When we eventually were able to get them to their feet again, we were able to agree with them in prayer about their needs. This happened again and again throughout our time of praying for people.

One of those encounters sticks out to me the most. A lady approached us and fell under the power of God. We helped her to her feet, and in tears she began to share all of the things that were happening in her life. She shared of family trouble, of losing her job, of being close to eviction, and then she added, "On top of that, I cannot even bend my knees to pray." This lady had some type of issue in her legs that limited her range of motion.

"That's a lot of problems," I said. "Let's pray."

As we prayed for her, the power of God flowed through her body. We finished praying, and I told her to begin to move and bend her knees. She was able to do so with complete flexibility. She dropped to her knees and began to worship God and thank Him for her healing. I observed her as tears flowed down her face, and I knew God was doing a greater internal work. The lady returned the next night and almost looked like a different person. She was so joyous. She called for us to come over. She walked up and down the stairs of the altar celebrating and exclaiming, "I haven't been able to do this for three months!" She was completely healed. She then shared how since we had prayed, a number of situations had turned around for her, including getting a new job. She added that she had lost her desire to live, but after her encounter with the glory of God, it had been restored.

I saw this lady a year later when I returned to Argentina. She stopped me and reminded me who she was. She said she had just encountered another job difficulty because she had done what was right. She was feeling down about the situation, because what had happened to her was unfair. But when she saw me walking by, she remembered her knee and then declared that if God did it before, He can do it again.

What God has placed in you and upon you is meant to be released and transmitted to others. Whether it is during a time of an especially strong anointing or during everyday life, you can release what God has divinely granted to you. The most common way that will happen is through the words you speak and the laying on of hands (see Mark 16:18). When I sense the anointing, to me the power most frequently feels like fire within my hands. However, there are times when I do not feel anything, but I know it is still there.

In August, as my schedule allows, I usually take an international trip to minister to a wonderful family of churches in South Africa and Zimbabwe. I had been blessed with the previous privilege of being their main conference speaker every time I attend. The Zimbabwean conference is composed of churches throughout Zimbabwe, and others from South Africa and other places travel to attend. When I minister there, I typically minister for five sessions. The last session is Sunday morning, and it always lasts over five hours. We have seen God do so many marvelous things during this time. During the Sunday service, I lay hands on and pray for all who are sick or have any type of ailment. As you can imagine, that takes a considerable amount of time if you are praying for a large group of people. Because of this, unless otherwise directed by the Spirit, I keep my prayers for each individual short.

Thus, when a young girl came to me with the complaint of having worms, I laid my hands on her head and said, "Burn it out, Jesus!" Afterward, I continued to pray for the rest who were in line. When the service ended, I went out to lunch with the pastor, and he began to share with me about the precious girl I had prayed for. He told me she went to the restroom after church, and there was no longer any evidence of worms. He then provided the background to the story that makes it even more miraculous.

This girl had lived in South Africa and somehow contracted worms. Her mother took her to various doctors, but they could not diagnose a specific cause. Finally, one doctor said that it was "cultural." The pastor said that "cultural" meant they believed it was caused by a witchdoctor somewhere. The grandmother heard about the meeting we were having in Zimbabwe, so she traveled to South Africa to pick up her granddaughter and brought her to the meeting in faith that she would be healed. When I prayed for her, the fire of God flowed through her body and eliminated what the devil had created. The fire of God is greater than anything the enemy and his forces can create, and it can handle things that doctors cannot diagnose. That fire is on the inside of you and needs to be released to the world around you.

Gifts, Operations, and Administrations

Often, when discussing the miraculous power of God, people focus on Paul's list in 1 Corinthians 12, which is commonly referred to as the nine gifts of the Spirit:

> *Now there are diversities of gifts, but the same Spirit. And there are differences of administrations, but the same Lord. And there are diversities of operations, but it is the same God which worketh all in all. But the manifestation of the Spirit is given to every man to profit withal. For to one is given by the Spirit the word of wisdom; to another the word of knowledge by the same Spirit; to another faith by the same Spirit; to another the gifts of healing by the same Spirit; to another the working of miracles; to another prophecy; to another discerning of spirits; to another divers kinds of tongues; to another the interpretation of tongues: But all these worketh that one and the selfsame Spirit, dividing to every man severally as he will* (1 Corinthians 12:4–11 KJV).

The apostle Paul described some of these gifts as operations, which means there are different ways that they operate. He also pointed out that there are differences of administration, meaning there are different ways of ministry and service. Here's the point he was driving home:

Although these abilities are various, they still all come from God. A person could operate in the same gift, but it could look different. The difference is not a problem; it just showcases the creativity of God in granting His believers miraculous abilities.

In Hebrews 6:5, the writer referred to these abilities as powers of the world or age to come. These futuristic abilities elevate a normal life beyond the limits of mere mortals. Some like to point out that the gifts of the Spirit only operate as the Spirit wills. This is very true (see 1 Cor. 12:11). However, He is more willing than we have given Him credit for, and He wants to manifest Himself through us. In 1 Corinthians 12:7, Paul said that these manifestations were given for a reason; they are the expressions, displays, and demonstrations of the Spirit. The manifestations go beyond gifts alone to include other evidences of the Spirit. These expressions, displays, demonstrations, and manifestations of the Spirit are given so that we can profit together and become better together. Believers are not meant to be islands; we need each other. As we all operate in the abilities, anointing, and graces that God has granted us, we will all get better together.

Ability to Produce Results

Nevertheless, brethren, I have written more boldly to you on some points, as reminding you, because of the grace given to me by God, that I might be a minister of Jesus Christ to the Gentiles, ministering the gospel of God, that the offering of the Gentiles might be acceptable, sanctified by the Holy Spirit (Romans 15:15–16).

Grace has over twenty different definitions and translations in the scripture. One of those definitions is "the power of the Holy Spirit," and it is synonymous with the anointing. In his writings, Paul talked about the grace, or the anointing of the Spirit, given to him to accomplish certain tasks. All believers have been graced in a general way, but also have specific graces and anointing upon their lives that grant them special abilities. One of the marvelous things about superheroes is the variety of powers and abilities they have. In a similar way, the body of Christ is composed of individuals with unique powers and abilities that flow from the grace of God.

Not every situation a believer encounters requires a superhuman act of miraculous power or authority; some situations require superhuman wisdom, innovation, and ability. The wisdom and grace of God grants some believers the ability to be innovative and produce results with God-ideas, concepts, and insights. This ability to produce results is a divine empowerment also known as the blessing that can rest upon people, their property, and whatever work or enterprise they are involved in. We see this in Deuteronomy 28:8, 12:

The Lord will command the blessing on you in your storehouses and in all to which you set your hand, and

He will bless you in the land which the Lord your God is giving you.... The Lord will open to you His good treasure, the heavens, to give the rain to your land in its season, and to bless all the work of your hand. You shall lend to many nations, but you shall not borrow.

When God placed Adam and Eve in charge of creation, in addition to granting them dominion, He empowered them with the blessing. The first words humankind ever heard were associated with the blessing. The scriptures say God blessed them *and* said unto them (see Gen. 1:28). The blessing empowerment preceded the instructions and delegation of authority. God also blessed Noah and his sons as they came off the ark. (see Gen. 9:1). God's first recorded promise to Abraham had to do with the empowerment of the blessing (see Gen. 12:1–3). Genesis shows how the blessing traveled from Abraham to Isaac and from Isaac to Jacob. Genesis 39 shows how the blessing enabled Joseph to be successful in unfair and distressing circumstances:

So it was, from the time that he had made him overseer of his house and all that he had, that the Lord blessed the Egyptian's house for Joseph's sake; and the blessing of the Lord was upon all that he had in the house and in the field.... The keeper of the prison did not look into anything that was under Joseph's authority, because the Lord was with him; and whatever he did, the Lord made it prosper (Genesis 39:5,23).

This empowerment continually operated through Joseph as he became prime minster of Egypt. The wisdom and skill of this empowerment preserved the Abrahamic line, the people of Egypt, and all who came to Egypt for provision.

God wanted the Israelites to know that it was His blessing that would produce wonderful results in their lives. In Deuteronomy 8, Moses reminded the people, saying:

> *Beware that you do not forget the Lord your God by not keeping His commandments, His judgments, and His statutes which I command you today, lest—when you have eaten and are full, and have built beautiful houses and dwell in them; and when your herds and your flocks multiply, and your silver and your gold are multiplied, and all that you have is multiplied; when your heart is lifted up, and you forget the Lord your God who brought you out of the land of Egypt, from the house of bondage; who led you through that great and terrible wilderness, in which were fiery serpents and scorpions and thirsty land where there was no water; who brought water for you out of the flinty rock; who fed you in the wilderness with manna, which your fathers did not know, that He might humble you and that He might test you, to do you good in the end—then you say in your heart, "My power and the might of my hand*

have gained me this wealth." And you shall remember the Lord your God, for it is He who gives you power to get wealth, that He may establish His covenant which He swore to your fathers, as it is this day (Deuteronomy 8:11–18).

According to Deuteronomy 8, the blessing was able to help the Israelites build and possess beautiful houses, multiply all of their livestock, and multiply their wealth. The empowerment of the blessing operated in the lives of Abraham's descendants through the centuries. It continually produced wonderful results for them.

This empowerment is also available to all who are born again. Galatians 3:13–14 says:

Christ has redeemed us from the curse of the law, having become a curse for us (for it is written, "Cursed is everyone who hangs on a tree"), that the blessing of Abraham might come upon the Gentiles in Christ Jesus, that we might receive the promise of the Spirit through faith.

All believers have the same access to the empowerment of the blessing as the physical descendants of Abraham did. The empowerment of the blessing produces superhuman results in the marketplace, on the sales floor, in boardrooms, and beyond.

> Progression in the ways of the Spirit and following the secrets outlined in this book leads people down a path where they can experience greater measures of grace and the blessing.

As there are levels and measures in the anointing, there are levels and measures in the grace that brings results and the blessing. Progression in the ways of the Spirit and following the secrets outlined in this book leads people down a path where they can experience greater measures of grace and the blessing. All believers are anointed. As such, believers should follow the example of Jesus and acknowledge the anointing on their individual lives on a regular basis. In the same way, believers need to acknowledge the grace and blessing on their lives.

If you are called to be a teacher, then you have a grace and blessing on your life to produce superhuman results in that arena. If you are called to be a corporate executive, then you have a grace and blessing on your life to produce superhuman results in that arena. If you are called to arts and entertainment, then you have a grace and blessing on your life to produce superhuman results. Whatever grace, anointing, and blessing is on your life, you need to daily acknowledge it with the words of your mouth. Here's a declaration to help you get started.

The Results Declaration

I am anointed. I am the blessed. The grace of God rests upon me. I have been anointed, empowered, blessed, and graced to produce superhuman results in (Say the field, career, or industry you are employed in or working toward). I do not settle for mere mortal results, because I am a new creation in Christ Jesus. The anointing, grace, and blessing of God are working strongly in my life and in everything that concerns me. The blessing on my life grants me God-ideas, concepts, insights, and disruptive innovations in my field. I yield to the voice of the Spirit of God. I hear His voice, and the voice of a stranger I will not follow. As I listen to and obey His voice, I will know what to do in every situation. Father, thank You for Your anointing, Your grace, and Your blessing.

> In the journey of the superhuman life, believers will encounter and have to face off with henchmen, villains, and supervillains.

Facing Supervillains

Every superhero has a foe, a supervillain that opposes him or her. Superman has Lex Luthor. Captain America has the Red Skull. The Fantastic Four have Doctor Doom.

Spider-man has the Green Goblin. The Avengers have Thanos. The Justice League has Darkseid. In the journey of the superhuman life, believers will encounter and have to face off with henchmen, villains, and supervillains. The original supervillains of the Old Testament times were the giants. When most people think of giants in the Bible, their minds race to David and Goliath. Let's examine this famous story in light of everything we have covered in this book. David was not on the battlefield that day to fight. He was Uber Eats or Door Dash. His father had sent him to bring food to his brothers, to their leader, and to find out how his brothers were doing. As David talked with his brothers, the giant began his daily taunt.

> *Then as he talked with them, there was the champion, the Philistine of Gath, Goliath by name, coming up from the armies of the Philistines; and he spoke according to the same words. So David heard them. And all the men of Israel, when they saw the man, fled from him and were dreadfully afraid. So the men of Israel said, "Have you seen this man who has come up? Surely he has come up to defy Israel; and it shall be that the man who kills him the king will enrich with great riches, will give him his daughter, and give his father's house exemption from taxes in Israel." Then David spoke to the men who stood by him, saying, "What shall be done for the man who kills this Philistine and takes away the reproach from Israel? For who is*

this uncircumcised Philistine, that he should defy the armies of the living God?" And the people answered him in this manner, saying, "So shall it be done for the man who kills him" (1 Samuel 17:23–27).

Goliath, the giant champion of Gath, taunted and challenged Israel every morning and evening for forty days. No one believed they could face him. No one was brave enough to attempt to challenge the Philistine warrior, who was more than nine feet tall. Even King Saul did not dare to challenge the warrior. The situation had grown so desperate that Saul had presented three substantial awards for any man who could defeat the giant. First, the successful warrior would be given a massive financial prize; second, his entire family would be exempt from paying taxes; third, the successful warrior would marry the princess and become part of the royal family.

David heard the threat of the giant, but he paid attention to the potential reward. He was so motivated by the reward that he asked the people to repeat it to him. What caused this anointed shepherd and musician to be confident that he could defeat a giant who had intimidated an entire army? David revealed the source of his confidence in verse 27 when he said, "Who is this uncircumcised Philistine, that he should defy the armies of the living God?" When David said the Philistine was uncircumcised, he was saying that the giant did not have a covenant with the living God. Circumcision was the sign of the old covenant. David, as a teenager, was so confident of his covenant and what his covenant made available to him that he believed he could take down the giant.

In the same way, believers must be confident in their new covenant and what God has made available to them as new creations in Christ Jesus. Dr. Billye Brim said it this way, "It's dangerous for us to preach power and never have any. One thing that will help you have power is to know who you are in Christ Jesus." When supervillain giants show up in your life, you cannot run and hide in terror like the Israelite army did. You have to become confident of your covenant and the vast resources that are within you because you are a child of the living God. This is why it is so very important that you rehearse and meditate on new creation realities. It is not about trying to build up confidence when the supervillain shows up; it is about meditating on these realities ahead of time so that when the supervillain shows up the confidence is already there. Let's return to the story of the teenage hero, David:

> *Now Eliab his oldest brother heard when he spoke to the men; and Eliab's anger was aroused against David, and he said, "Why did you come down here? And with whom have you left those few sheep in the wilderness? I know your pride and the insolence of your heart, for you have come down to see the battle." And David said, "What have I done now? Is there not a cause?" Then he turned from him toward another*

and said the same thing; and these people answered him as the first ones did (1 Samuel 17:28–30).

As David was investigating the reward, his oldest brother became enraged. He insulted David and belittled his occupation. He accused him with false accusations. Although all of this was coming from someone who should have supported him, David was not moved or intimidated. He responded with, "Is there not a cause?" Is there not a cause for you to become the superhuman you were born again to be? Is there not a cause for you to rise up and defeat the supervillains that are intimidating your family and community? Is there not a cause for believers to walk into the fullness of their redemption and grasp every single new creation reality? Is there not a cause for you? David had a cause and a covenant, and so do you. David was anointed (see 1 Sam. 16), and so are you. Let's return to our young hero who was equipped in a similar way to us:

> *Now when the words which David spoke were heard, they reported them to Saul; and he sent for him. Then David said to Saul, "Let no man's heart fail because of him; your servant will go and fight with this Philistine." And Saul said to David, "You are not able to go against this Philistine to fight with him; for you are a youth, and he a man of war from his youth." But David said to Saul, "Your servant used to keep his father's sheep, and when a lion or a bear came and took a lamb out of the flock, I went out after it and*

struck it, and delivered the lamb from its mouth; and when it arose against me, I caught it by its beard, and struck and killed it. Your servant has killed both lion and bear; and this uncircumcised Philistine will be like one of them, seeing he has defied the armies of the living God." Moreover David said, "The Lord, who delivered me from the paw of the lion and from the paw of the bear, He will deliver me from the hand of this Philistine." And Saul said to David, "Go, and the Lord be with you" (1 Samuel 17:31–37).

Saul was ecstatic. Someone would finally face the giant of Gath. He summoned David, but when David arrived, Saul was surprised by what he saw. He told David he could not face the Philistine, because he was too young. He said Goliath had been a warrior since he was a teenager. The confident, courageous, anointed hero with a covenant explained to the king the reason why he knew he could defeat the giant. David recounted the faithfulness of God that he had seen displayed when he battled a lion and a bear. The shepherd was not looking for a fight, but a fight came and found him. When the lion and bear stole a lamb from David's flock, he pursued the beasts, killed them, and rescued his lambs. The flock was under David's dominion. He understood who he was because of his covenant. He knew who his God was, and he knew he was anointed. This understanding granted David the boldness needed to pursue, conquer, and rescue.

Your testimony is powerful; your story of how God has proved Himself faithful to you in the past will strengthen you so you can victoriously confront the challenges of your future. In your superhuman journey, you will confront henchmen and villains, just as David faced a lion and a bear. These are threatening challenges that you can overcome, and fighting them will train you for dealing with super-villains. Consistently resisting and exercising the power of dominion over small challenges prepares you to resist and overcome larger situations. Consistently acknowledging and operating in the miraculous power of God prepares you for special and unique manifestations of His glory and power. Consistently applying the grace and the blessing on your life to situations in the workplace will prepare you for disruptive innovations and shifting industries.

As I have shared throughout this book, the journey is a process. Every step prepares you for the next step. Reverend Rick Renner once told me, "The steps of obedience you take today lay the groundwork for the steps of obedience you take tomorrow." Your superhuman journey is unique to you; as you walk with God and operate by these seven secrets, you will continually grow stronger and be able to conquer greater challenges. As you do this, you will grow in confidence and will be able to declare that the same God who delivered you from the henchmen and the villains will deliver you from the supervillains. Now, let's read about how our hero took on his first supervillain, Goliath the giant Philistine warrior from Gath:

So Saul clothed David with his armor, and he put a bronze helmet on his head; he also clothed him with a coat of mail. David fastened his sword to his armor and tried to walk, for he had not tested them. And David said to Saul, "I cannot walk with these, for I have not tested them." So David took them off. Then he took his staff in his hand; and he chose for himself five smooth stones from the brook, and put them in a shepherd's bag, in a pouch which he had, and his sling was in his hand. And he drew near to the Philistine (1 Samuel 17:38–40).

Saul's armor did not fit David. However, the armor that God has given to every single believer fits them perfectly (see Eph. 6:10–18). Why did David pick up five stones from the brook? The scripture tells us that Goliath had other giant warrior relatives who would battle the Israelites (see 2 Sam. 21:18–22). David was prepared for whatever the battle would bring. Consistently putting into practice the seven secrets shared in this book and actively progressing in your superhuman journey will prepare you for whatever supervillain or battle you may encounter.

So the Philistine came, and began drawing near to David, and the man who bore the shield went before him. And when the Philistine looked about and saw David, he disdained him; for he was only a youth, ruddy and good-looking. So the Philistine said to David, "Am I a dog, that you come to me with sticks?"

And the Philistine cursed David by his gods. And the Philistine said to David, "Come to me, and I will give your flesh to the birds of the air and the beasts of the field!" Then David said to the Philistine, "You come to me with a sword, with a spear, and with a javelin. But I come to you in the name of the Lord of hosts, the God of the armies of Israel, whom you have defied. This day the Lord will deliver you into my hand, and I will strike you and take your head from you. And this day I will give the carcasses of the camp of the Philistines to the birds of the air and the wild beasts of the earth, that all the earth may know that there is a God in Israel. Then all this assembly shall know that the Lord does not save with sword and spear; for the battle is the Lord's, and He will give you into our hands." So it was, when the Philistine arose and came and drew near to meet David, that David hurried and ran toward the army to meet the Philistine (1 Samuel 17:41–48).

As is typical of so many supervillains, Goliath gave a speech about his plans and how he would defeat David. He despised David's youth and appearance. David was not intimidated by the Philistine, his words, or his cursing. David was not silent. You should not be silent when running at giants or facing down supervillains. David recognized the weapons of his enemy, but he declared that he was facing off with the Philistine in the name and authority of the Lord of Hosts, the God of Angel Armies. David was operating in the power of dominion that he had learned when he dealt with the lion and the bear. He was using the delegated authority he had because of his covenant. Remember, when you face off with supervillains, you are the one who has the greater authority and power. Your authority and power flow from the Most High God, who has also assigned angels to assist you in all of your ways.

Just like that, the battle was on! The giant charged at David, and David ran toward the Philistine.

> *Then David put his hand in his bag and took out a stone; and he slung it and struck the Philistine in his forehead, so that the stone sank into his forehead, and he fell on his face to the earth. So David prevailed over the Philistine with a sling and a stone, and struck the Philistine and killed him. But there was no sword in the hand of David. Therefore David ran and stood over the Philistine, took his sword and drew it out of its sheath and killed him, and cut off his head with it. And when the Philistines saw that their champion was dead, they fled* (1 Samuel 17:49–51).

David defeated his giant just like you will defeat your supervillain. Did you know that David was not the only giant slayer in the Bible? Throughout the Old Testament we find stories of battles in which the children of Israel overcame giants and their armies. Moses slayed the giant King Og (see Josh. 13:12). Caleb also overcame giants (see Judg. 1:20). Likewise, David's nephew and warriors in

David's army took down giants (see 2 Sam. 21). Even the Ammonites and the Edomites conquered giants (see Deut. 2:20–21). What did all of these people have in common? They were part of Abraham's family, and so are you (see Gal. 3:29). The family they were born into qualified them to become warriors who defeated giants. The family you were born again into qualifies you to defeat every supervillain you may encounter. You are no longer a mere mortal.

Finally, My Brothers and Sisters

Near the end of his letter to the Ephesians, Paul wrote, "Finally, my brethren, be strong in the Lord and in the power of His might" (Ephesians 6:10). As I conclude this book, I am reminded of Paul's closing exhortation to the Ephesians. He told them to be strong in the Lord and in the power of His might. The phrase "be strong" is a reminder to tap into and access the miraculous power of God that has been made available to all new creations in Christ Jesus. This phrase is the same phrase that was used in ancient Greek mythological writings to describe Hercules and others who were empowered by the gods to achieve superhuman feats. Paul employed the same language to remind believers that the power they have access to will enable them to accomplish superhuman results.

Remember, you have been empowered to live a superhuman life; you have been granted power far beyond mere mortals. Do not access this power every once in a while; access it daily so that you can become strong in this power.

As the scripture says, we are to "be strong in the Lord." This superhuman strength flows from our relationship with Him. It reminds me of Daniel 11:32, which says that those who "know their God shall be strong, and carry out great exploits." Exploits are bold and daring achievements that require great courage, skill, or strength.

The words *power* and *might* in Ephesians 6:10 showcase the dominion of God's ability. God has granted you dominion and superhuman abilities. Do not settle for infrequent or low-level manifestation of dominion and abilities. Be strong in this area, constantly grow, and reach for the greatest heights of what God has made available to you as the redeemed of the Lord. As you do, you will do exploits.

Superheroes are popular because they inspire people to dream and imagine about what is possible. Stories of superheroes tap into an internal desire to become more than we have been in the past. Superheroes are also wildly popular because people need heroes. We live in a world of intense situations created by human failure and demonic pressure. We live in a world of seemingly impossible challenges. These challenges, situations, and pressures have presented themselves as giants and supervillains. The world needs heroes. Will you be who God made you to be? Will you put on your proverbial cape and rise to the challenge, or will you hide behind a disguise like Clark Kent? This generation needs you to be who you were born again to be—the new creation, the child of the living God.

As you progress on your superhuman journey with hunger, reverence, an understanding of new creation realities, faith, love, the mind of Christ, and the power of God, your life will impact the lives of many. Yes, you will see personal benefits of pursuing this path, but it will also change the lives of those you come into contact with. They will be delivered from the supervillains who oppress them because of your faithfulness to answer the call, and you will be able to introduce them to our wonderful Jesus.

Look—your bat-signal is in the sky. It is time for you to go ahead in your superhuman journey. As you step forward and consistently apply what you learned in this book, you will learn more and experience the greatness of what God has made available to all of His children. I am praying for you. I pray this book has awakened you to what God has made available to you. I pray you will not forget what you learned. I pray you will be filled with strength and boldness. I pray you will answer the call and no longer live as a mere mortal, but as the superhuman you were born again and anointed to be. Enjoy your journey and adventure.

In His love,

KERRICK

ABOUT KERRICK BUTLER II

Kerrick A. R. Butler II serves as Senior Pastor of Faith Christian Center headquartered in Austell, Georgia, with satellite campuses throughout the metro Atlanta area. He is a graduate of Word of Faith Bible Training Center and Oral Roberts University. Kerrick believes wholeheartedly in sharing the message of Jesus through creative avenues to help readers apply Bible truths to their everyday lives. Kerrick, his wife, Racquel, and their beautiful family reside in the metro Atlanta area.

OUR VISION

Proclaiming the truth and the power of the Gospel of Jesus Christ with excellence. Challenging Christians to live victoriously, grow spiritually, know God intimately.

Connect with us on

Facebook @ HarrisonHousePublishers

and Instagram @ HarrisonHousePublishing

so you can stay up to date with news

about our books and our authors.

Visit us at www.harrisonhouse.com

for a complete product listing as well as

monthly specials for wholesale distribution.